PUBLISHED FOR THE ELIZABETHAN CLUB

OF YALE UNIVERSITY IN HONOR OF THE

FOUR HUNDREDTH ANNIVERSARY OF

SHAKESPEARE'S BIRTH

The Elizabethan Club Series 3

SHAKESPEARE'S

POEMS

VENUS AND ADONIS

LUCRECE

THE PASSIONATE PILGRIM

THE PHOENIX AND TURTLE

THE SONNETS

A LOVER'S COMPLAINT

A Facsimile of the Earliest Editions

PUBLISHED FOR THE ELIZABETHAN CLUB

New Haven and London, Yale University Press 1964

CONTENTS

PREFACE

SHAKESPEARE was known to Elizabethans not only as a dramatist but also as a writer of Ovidian love poetry. In 1598 Francis Meres, comparing English poets with those of Greece, Rome, and contemporary Italy, wrote that "the sweete wittie soule of Ovid lives in mellifluous and hony-tongued Shakespeare, witnes his *Venus and Adonis,* his *Lucrece,* his sugred *Sonnets* among his private friends, &c." The poems he mentioned were the most famous and the best. *Venus and Adonis* had already gone through four editions, and a second edition of *Lucrece* appeared in the same year as Meres' statement. The *Sonnets,* as he indicated, were being circulated in manuscript.

As part of its celebration of the four hundredth anniversary of Shakespeare's birth, the Elizabethan Club at Yale has reproduced in this volume the earliest extant editions of all of Shakespeare's nondramatic poetry. Four of these are quartos and one is a very small octavo. The copies of *Lucrece* and the *Sonnets* presented here are in the collection of the Elizabethan Club. For permission to reproduce the others we make grateful acknowledgment: to the Bodleian Library for *Venus and Adonis;* to the Folger Shakespeare Library for excerpts from the fragmentary first edition of *The Passionate Pilgrim* and for "The Phoenix and Turtle" from *Love's Martyr;* to the Henry E. Huntington Library and Art Gallery for the second (the earliest extant complete) edition of *The Passionate Pilgrim.*

Both *Venus and Adonis* and *Lucrece,* the first two of these poems, were dedicated to Shakespeare's patron, the Earl of Southampton. They are more carefully printed than the rest, and it is generally accepted that Shakespeare saw them through the press. It is unlikely that he did this for any other of his published works. He does not appear to have been directly responsible for the publication of any of the other poems, while the plays, not regarded as strictly literary productions in Shakespeare's day, were the property of the actors. It is a reasonable assumption, then, that the texts of these two early poems represent more exactly than any other printed texts what Shakespeare actually wrote. As often happened, a few corrections were made in the process of printing, though uncorrected sheets were not discarded. Some of these corrections may have been made by Shakespeare rather than the printer. For example, in lines 125–26 of *Lucrece* "himselfe betakes" and "wakes" were apparently changed to "themselues betake" and "wake" (either reading being grammatically acceptable at the time). Here the Elizabethan Club copy has the earlier reading, as can be seen on page 69; modern editions usually give the later one, preserved in other copies.

The Bodleian copy of the first edition of *Venus and Adonis* (1593) is the only one known to exist. Of the first edition of *Lucrece* (1594) there are eleven known copies, two of them imperfect. The Elizabethan Club copy is one of the nine perfect exemplars. The title *Lucrece,* as it appears on the title page, may have been one of Shakespeare's second thoughts, for the heading at the beginning of the poem and the running heads throughout read "The Rape of Lucrece." Since the poem was presumably printed before the title page, the longer title was probably the one in Shakespeare's manuscript. In the sixth edition (1616) it was put on the title page and has become in modern times the title more often used. However, Meres called the poem *Lucrece.*

The Passionate Pilgrim was a shady publishing venture by William Jaggard—morally shady and also obscure in origin, for despite much research it is still not clear exactly what happened. Presumably Jaggard got hold of a commonplace book of the sort in which Elizabethan gentlemen copied poems and sayings they admired. In this one there were apparently some poems by Shakespeare, including two of the "sugred *Sonnets*" which we know from Meres were then circulating in manuscript. Shakespeare was sufficiently popular to make a volume of his poems an attractive undertaking, and Jaggard brought the collection out, probably in 1599, with Shakespeare's name on the title page. Five of the poems are undoubtedly Shakespeare's: the two sonnets (numbers I and II) which later appeared in slightly different versions as numbers 138 and 144 of Shakespeare's *Sonnets* (1609); and two more sonnets (numbers III and V) and a song (number XVI) which, again in slightly different versions, had been used in *Love's Labor's Lost,* published the preceding year. How many of the other poems may have been attributed to Shakespeare in Jaggard's manuscript we cannot tell, but he must at least have known that two of the poems (numbers VIII and XX) had just been published by his brother in a volume of Richard Barnfield's poetry entitled *The Encomion of Lady Pecunia*. The stanzas that appear as number XIX ("Live with me and be my love" and "Love's Answer") were printed for the first time in *The Passionate Pilgrim;* in 1600 they appeared in *England's Helicon* as portions of the popular companion-poems, "The Passionate Shepherd to his Love" and "The Nymph's Reply," where the first poem is attributed to Marlowe, and the second to "Ignoto" (the attribution to Raleigh stems from Izaak Walton's statement in 1653). A variant version of "Venus with Adonis sitting by her" (number XI) had been published in 1596 in Bartholomew Griffin's *Fidessa.*

It is impossible to credit Jaggard's good faith, especially since, in a third edition of *The Passionate Pilgrim,* he included some poems he had already printed and knew to be by Thomas Heywood. Nevertheless, it is possible that more than five of the poems in this collection were written by Shakespeare, whether or not he intended them for publication.

The printed editions of *The Passionate Pilgrim* present still further problems. The earliest complete edition known to survive is the second (1599), of which the Huntington copy, reproduced here, is the better of two known copies. Its pages have been severely trimmed, however, and in the case of one poem, number XV, the last words in four lines have been cut into. They are: *could see* (l. 3), *did fight* (l. 5), *gaine* (l. 10), and *disdaine* (l. 11). A copy in the Folger Library is made up of two gatherings (B and D) of this edition and two (A and C) of the first edition, otherwise unknown, of which, however, no title page survives, so that its date can only be conjectured. It was probably published in 1599 also. The second edition was based upon the first but differed from it in various ways. A second title page was introduced midway in gathering C: *Sonnets To sundry notes of Musicke*—with no indication of author. (Was this in response to a protest by Shakespeare?) And the arrangement of the first edition was not followed page for page. In one case stanzas of a poem were printed in a different order. As was usual with Elizabethan reprintings, punctuation and spelling were frequently altered. One difference between the two editions lay in the use made of the reverse sides of the leaves. The printer of the first edition placed the beginning of each poem on the right side of the leaf, but continued it, if necessary, on the reverse side. The printer of the second edition used only the right side until he reached the last two poems, which he printed on both sides to avoid adding another sheet. Because of the changes in arrangement the composite copy in the Folger Library does not provide a complete text: parts of some poems are duplicated; parts of others are omitted (for a full account of this copy of *The Passionate Pilgrim* see the admirable introduction by J. Q. Adams to the facsimile reprint listed in our bibliography). Since this copy contains all that is known to remain of the first edition, however, the pages containing the poems known to be by Shakespeare have been reproduced in this volume following the complete second edition.

Shakespeare's poem on "The Phoenix and Turtle" with his name printed at the end of it appeared in a volume of poetry called *Love's Martyr* (1601). To the title poem by Robert Chester, which made use of the legend of the phoenix and the turtle, were added, as the title page announced, *"some new compositions, of severall moderne Writers whose names are subscribed to their severall workes, upon the first Subject: viz. the* Phoenix *and* Turtle." Among the "modern writers" were Ben Jonson and George Chapman along with Shakespeare; the section of the book containing their contributions was preceded by a second title page. Both title pages and Shakespeare's poem are reproduced here from the Folger copy of the first edition. Only one other copy is known to exist.

Thomas Thorpe published *Shake-speares Sonnets. Never before Imprinted* (1609) with no more authorization, in all probability, than Jaggard had for *The Passionate Pilgrim*. In this case, however, there is no reason to doubt the correctness of the ascription, and except for the two sonnets in Jaggard's volume, it was true that these poems had never before been imprinted. Thorpe's dedication of his book to "Mr. W. H." has been the subject of seemingly endless controversy. Since Thorpe calls him "the onlie begetter" of the sonnets, it is usually supposed that this person must be the young friend to whom the first 126 sonnets are addressed (for the controversy, see the books listed in our bibliography).

Thirteen copies of the first edition of the *Sonnets* are known today, three of them imperfect. The title pages indicate that some were to be sold by William Aspley and some by John Wright. The Elizabethan Club copy, in perfect condition except that a few headlines have been cut into, has the Wright imprint. After the sonnets Thorpe printed a poem called "A

Lover's Complaint," which he specifically attributed to Shakespeare. It belongs with several of the poems in *The Passionate Pilgrim* in the category of works which may be "early Shakespeare."

⌘

The aim of this volume, then, is to provide convenient and reliable facsimiles of the earliest extant printings of Shakespeare's nondramatic poems. Full and admirable annotation, both textual and explanatory, will be found in the editions listed at the close of this preface, some of which are easily available at very small expense. It has seemed to us worthwhile simply to reproduce the poems: first, for the strong historical interest these early printings justifiably possess; and secondly, for the more essential function of providing original materials for use in conjunction with the many modern editions available. The basic interest of the present volume, we believe, will emerge through a close comparison of these early printings with the modernized texts in which we usually read the poems.

Modernized texts of course have their indispensable usefulness: by removing the accidents of antiquity they create an effect of bringing the reader easily, directly, and familiarly into the presence of the poem. But at the same time a danger arises when, as with Shakespeare, these texts become second nature to us, when they become almost the only texts we ever use. Familiarity breeds consent: after years of reading and teaching Shakespeare's sonnets, for example, in a modernized version, we may tend to overlook the extent to which the poem we are reading is a version, an editorial interpretation, of the poem. The effect of moving easily into the presence of the poem is in part an illusion: what we read is not quite the poem, but something that includes spellings, punctuation marks, and even emendations that may keep us some distance from the original poem.

On the other hand it is certainly true that a return to the earliest editions may bring us no closer: for then we are at the mercy of the Elizabethan printer, who in turn may have been following copy several times removed from the author's original. Moreover, there are the many distracting practices of early printing: the strange, erratic spelling; the apparently inconsistent punctuation, with all the familiar marks used in a way quite different from our own; and also certain typographical conventions that we can never perhaps completely absorb: the long "s" which resembles "f," the medial "u" for "v," the initial "v" for "u," and the use of "i" for modern "j"—symbols so pervasive and insignificant that they are better normalized in typographical reprints of old-spelling texts, as in the handsome "Nonesuch Shakespeare." But if one admits this small degree of modernization, why not more? Why not normalize Elizabethan "then" to modern "than"? And why bother to reproduce such misleading and insignificant spellings as "beare" for "bier," "were" for "wear," "cauld" for "call'd," and "could" for "cold"? It may well seem mere sentimentality to urge the retention of spellings that offer no service to pronunciation, rhythm, and meaning.

A difficulty arises, however, when we begin the effort to discriminate among significant and insignificant spelling. The best way to see the problem is to look at a representative example, the famous sonnet 106, first in the modernized version of the influential Oxford Shakespeare, edited by W. J. Craig, and then in the version of 1609, with "s," "u," "v," "i," and "j" normalized:

> When in the chronicle of wasted time
> I see descriptions of the fairest wights,
> And beauty making beautiful old rime,
> In praise of ladies dead and lovely knights,
> 5 Then, in the blazon of sweet beauty's best,
> Of hand, of foot, of lip, of eye, of brow,
> I see their antique pen would have express'd
> Even such a beauty as you master now.
> So all their praises are but prophecies
> 10 Of this our time, all you prefiguring;
> And, for they look'd but with divining eyes,
> They had not skill enough your worth to sing:
> > For we, which now behold these present days,
> > Have eyes to wonder, but lack tongues to praise.

> When in the Chronicle of wasted time,
> I see discriptions of the fairest wights,
> And beautie making beautifull old rime,
> In praise of Ladies dead, and lovely Knights,
> 5 Then in the blazon of sweet beauties best,
> Of hand, of foote, of lip, of eye, of brow,

I see their antique Pen would have exprest,
Even such a beauty as you maister now.
So all their praises are but prophesies
10 Of this our time, all you prefiguring,
And for they look'd but with devining eyes,
They had not still enough your worth to sing:
    For we which now behold these present dayes,
    Have eyes to wonder, but lack toungs to praise.

Here the old punctuation presents little difficulty: commas occur in places where we should not nowadays expect to find them, but the pauses they suggest are possible and appropriate; the commas are not erratic, but are placed according to another system of notation. Craig's revised punctuation, however, seems to ask for pauses that spoil the flow of the lines: the commas after "Then" (line 5), "And" (line 11), and "we" (line 13) seem disruptive, and the semicolon at the end of line 10 enforces a heavy pause that breaks the natural unity of this quatrain—a unity that flows from the allusion to typological prophecy, in the old manner of biblical interpretation (with an echo of 1 Corinthians 13).

Meanwhile the use of capitalization is discreet and functional in the old version: "Chronicle" suggests some specific old book, such as the "Chronicles" of Hall or Holinshed; "Ladies" and "Knights" deserve their formal distinction; and "Pen" is central to the poem's theme of praise. Aside from two spellings that indicate contraction ("exprest" and "look'd"), two others may have some slight significance for pronunciation: "discriptions," "devining"; while "maister" retains the vestiges of its ancient derivation from *magister*. In line 5 the change from "beauties" to "beauty's" prejudges and delimits the meaning: "beauties" may be either singular or plural possessive, or perhaps not possessive at all, but a plural noun, modified adjectively by "best."

The most interesting problem, however, lies in the emendation of "still" to "skill" (line 12), first made in the eighteenth century, and followed in most of the modern editions. This is one of many plausible emendations scattered throughout the modern editions of Shakespeare's poems, emendations which a return to the original text may often lead us to question. For "still" makes sense here in the meaning "yet"; while it is also possible that "still" may be a variant spelling of "style" (or "stile," as we find it spelled elsewhere in the *Sonnets:* e.g. 32.14). The *Oxford English Dictionary* lists the spellings "still," "styill," or "stylle" as current spellings for "style" in the sixteenth century; an Elizabethan would also have been aware that "stile" could indicate a writing instrument, a pen, as in the derivation from *stilus* (*OED,* "style" *sb.* 1).

To retain all the old spellings that have a possible significance would thus in this sonnet mean retaining most of the unusual spellings; to modernize the remainder ("beautie," "beautifull," "foote," "prophesies," "dayes," "toungs") would create no particular loss—and no particular benefit, since these spellings are not at all confusing. On principle, it seems better to modernize Shakespeare entirely, or not to modernize at all (except for "s," "u," "v," "i," and "j"), for either version of the poem will then maintain a general unity in its effect. If the total effect of modernization is to create an impression of easy access, the total effect of old spelling is the opposite—and it is of course this aspect of strangeness that has led to the practice of modernization. It is sometimes argued that we do wrong to accentuate a poem's antiquity through the maintenance of the old spelling; yet from another standpoint one of the prime virtues of an old-spelling text lies exactly in the fact that it calls attention to the poem's antiquity, maintains by its old spelling a constant reminder that meanings may also have changed. The illusion of familiarity in a modernized text may be as misleading as the strangeness of antiquity is puzzling; and what is at first puzzling may become fascinating and ultimately fruitful, as in the case of "still" above. We need to grasp both the modernity and the antiquity of the text, in order to approach that ideal object, the true poem, with a fair measure of accuracy.

In that approach the old punctuation may be of the utmost interest, as Empson has pointed out, since the old use of commas allows for "an interpenetrating and, as it were, fluid unity, in which phrases will go either with the sentence before or after and there is no break in the movement of the thought" (*Seven Types of Ambiguity,* 2d ed., 1947, p. 50). Striking examples of this effect may be found in Sonnet 81 (discussed by Empson), or in the opening of Sonnet 60, where the usual modern semicolon at the end of the second line spoils the old fluency (while the usual change from "pibled" to "pebbled" removes the assonance with "minuites"):

Like as the waves make towards the pebbled shore,
So do our minutes hasten to their end;
Each changing place with that which goes before,
In sequent toil all forwards do contend.

Like as the waves make towards the pibled shore,
So do our minuites hasten to their end,
Each changing place with that which goes before,
In sequent toile all forwards do contend.

Such fluidity, however, is not the only important characteristic of the old punctuation, which is frequently precise and strongly directive, in places where such delimitation serves a purpose. One can find several examples in the original version of the subtly ironic Sonnet 57, where the parentheses help to develop a tone of mock politeness, and where the strong punctuation of the opening quatrain leads the reader to slow up and savor the undercurrent of bitterness:

Being your slave what should I doe but tend,
Upon the houres, and times of your desire?
I have no precious time at al to spend;
Nor services to doe til you require.
5 Nor dare I chide the world without end houre,
Whilst I (my soveraine) watch the clock for you,
Nor thinke the bitternesse of absence sowre,
When you have bid your servant once adieue.
Nor dare I question with my jealious thought,
10 Where you may be, or your affaires suppose,
But like a sad slave stay and thinke of nought
Save where you are, how happy you make those.
So true a foole is love, that in your Will,
(Though you doe any thing) he thinkes no ill.

A comparison with Craig's version will show how much the whole poem loses in its modern dress:

Being your slave, what should I do but tend
Upon the hours and times of your desire?
I have no precious time at all to spend,

Nor services to do, till you require.

5 Nor dare I chide the world-without-end hour
Whilst I, my sovereign, watch the clock for you,
Nor think the bitterness of absence sour
When you have bid your servant once adieu;
Nor dare I question with my jealous thought
10 Where you may be, or your affairs suppose,
But, like a sad slave, stay and think of nought,
Save, where you are how happy you make those.
   So true a fool is love that in your will,
   Though you do anything, he thinks no ill.

The loss of the capital in "Will" (line 13) removes an emphasis upon the pun on Shakespeare's name; the intrusive commas of Craig in lines 11–12 diminish the rushing impact of the old version, while even the small change from "jealious" to "jealous" removes an assonance with "question" in line 9.

Shakespeare's sonnets move with such a delicate action that even the smallest jar is likely to produce some loss in accuracy. Thus in Sonnet 71 the opening quatrain in modern editions usually reads:

No longer mourn for me when I am dead
Than you shall hear the surly sullen bell
Give warning to the world that I am fled
From this vile world, with vilest worms to dwell:

But the last line in 1609 reads:

From this vile world with vildest wormes to dwell:

The spelling "vilde" is of course only a common variant of "vile"; but here the "ld," echoing "world" and linking with the "d" in "dwell," helps to create a powerful unity in the line, unbroken by any comma. Meanwhile the shift in the line to a harsher pronunciation gives a particular emphasis to "vildest," enforcing the ironic surprise of the line: the pious, conventional thought of fleeing "this vile world" is shattered by the thought that death may lead to something worse: extinction; "vildest" thus foreshadows the shudder of line 10: "When I (perhaps) compounded am with clay."

Among the many other valuable effects of the old versions, one should note especially the interesting parenthesis of Sonnet 29:

(Like to the Larke at breake of daye arising)

and the rare and therefore striking use of italics, as in the *"Rose"* of Sonnet 1, the *"Intrim"* of Sonnet 56, or the *"Informer"* of Sonnet 125; and the frequently striking effects of the discreet capitalization, as in "You are my All the world" (Sonnet 112), "thou the Master Mistris of my passion" (Sonnet 20), "When to the Sessions of sweet silent thought" (Sonnet 30), or the couplet of Sonnet 109:

For nothing this wide Universe I call,
Save thou my Rose, in it thou art my all.

This is not to say that the early editions are flawless: there are certainly a good many typographical errors, such as the notorious repetition of "my sinfull earth" in Sonnet 146, the "rn'wd quiers" of Sonnet 73, the two misprints in the last line of Sonnet 23, or the commas that sometimes occur at the ends of sonnets. Still, according to the standards of Elizabethan printing, the first editions of *Venus and Adonis, Lucrece,* and the *Sonnets* seem to be done with a fair amount of care. If one tries to assess the amount of obvious and indubitable error in the *Sonnets,* for example, most readers would perhaps agree upon no more than fifty examples in the wording—and these would include the fifteen places where the printer (perhaps following some difficulty in the manuscript) seems to have printed "their" for "thy." Most of the slips are not gross, for they usually involve no more than a single letter. And the punctuation, as we have suggested, seems to be quite carefully done. *Venus and Adonis* and *Lucrece,* being printed for presentation to a noble patron, were presumably set up from a good manuscript provided by the author himself. As for the *Sonnets,* we cannot say what sort of manuscript lay behind the printing of 1609; but the effective way in which the capitals and italics are handled may suggest that the printer is following closely a manuscript of good authority, even to the point of including fifteen lines in what may have been an imperfectly revised version of Sonnet 99.

Finally, one should note how well, in the *Sonnets* of 1609, the rarity of exclamation points and the fluency of comma punctuation accord with

the characteristic action in many of the greater sonnets: the action that
Shakespeare describes in the famous lines of Sonnet 64:

> Ruine hath taught me thus to ruminate
> That Time will come and take my love away.

To ruminate: "To revolve, turn over and over in the mind" (*OED, v.* 1);
or in the literal Elizabethan sense, derived from *ruminare:* "To chew the
cud" (*OED, v.* 3). Chewing the cud of thought, revolving the thought over
and over, in different imagistic manifestations, not by logical determination, but by subtle indefinable association, until the inward action has been
thoroughly played out, and the couplet, in muted conclusion, may sum
up the significance—such is the action in many of the greatest of the sonnets. How deeply that brooding, ruminative action may be disturbed by
modernization, and how well it may be maintained in the old text, may be
amply illustrated by comparing two versions of Sonnet 90, the first in the
heavily stopped, logical, oratorical punctuation of Craig, and the second in
the flexible, flowing punctuation of 1609:

> Then hate me when thou wilt; if ever, now;
> Now, while the world is bent my deeds to cross,
> Join with the spite of fortune, make me bow,
> And do not drop in for an after-loss:
> 5 Ah! do not, when my heart hath 'scap'd this sorrow,
> Come in the rearward of a conquer'd woe;
> Give not a windy night a rainy morrow,
> To linger out a purpos'd overthrow.
> If thou wilt leave me, do not leave me last,
> 10 When other petty griefs have done their spite,
> But in the onset come: so shall I taste
> At first the very worst of fortune's might;
>   And other strains of woe, which now seem woe,
>   Compar'd with loss of thee will not seem so.

> Then hate me when thou wilt, if ever, now,
> Now while the world is bent my deeds to crosse,
> Joyne with the spight of fortune, make me bow,
> And doe not drop in for an after losse:

5 Ah doe not, when my heart hath scapte this sorrow,
  Come in the rereward of a conquerd woe,
  Give not a windy night a rainie morrow,
  To linger out a purposd over-throw.
  If thou wilt leave me, do not leave me last,
10 When other pettie griefes have done their spight,
  But in the onset come, so s[h]all I taste
  At first the very worst of fortunes might.
     And other straines of woe, which now seeme woe,
     Compar'd with losse of thee, will not seeme so.

We hope that this facsimile edition will enable a wide range of readers to estimate the value of such comparisons for all of Shakespeare's non-dramatic poetry.

THE PUBLICATIONS COMMITTEE
OF THE ELIZABETHAN CLUB:

James M. Osborn, *Chairman*
Louis L. Martz
Eugene M. Waith

New Haven, Connecticut
April 23, 1964

SELECTED BIBLIOGRAPHY

EDITIONS

Sonnets, Variorum Edition, ed. Hyder Edward Rollins, 2 vols., Philadelphia, Lippincott, 1944. Indispensable for thorough study of the *Sonnets;* vol. 1 contains text, full textual notes, and elaborate commentary on each sonnet; vol. 2 contains discussions of special problems and controversies.

Sonnets, Arden Edition, ed. C. Knox Pooler, London, Methuen, 1918. To be superseded in this series by the forthcoming new edition by Winifred Nowottny.

Sonnets, Pelican Edition, ed. Douglas Bush and Alfred Harbage, Baltimore, Penguin Books, 1961. Attractive paperback, with excellent brief annotation.

Sonnets, Crofts Classics Edition, ed. Hyder Edward Rollins, New York, Appleton-Century-Crofts, 1951. Handy paperback, with good minimal annotation.

Poems, Variorum Edition, ed. Hyder Edward Rollins, Philadelphia, Lippincott, 1938. With indispensable notes and commentary.

Poems, Arden Edition, ed. F. T. Prince, London, Methuen; Cambridge, Mass., Harvard University Press, 1960. With excellent introduction and ample notes.

The Passionate Pilgrim, ed. J. Q. Adams, New York, Scribner's, 1939. A facsimile of the Folger copy, with a definitive introduction, dealing with the early editions.

Songs and Poems, ed. Edward Hubler, New York, McGraw-Hill, 1959. Contains all the nondramatic poems, as well as songs from Shakespeare's plays; with very helpful annotation.

STUDIES

Bradbrook, M. C., *Shakespeare and Elizabethan Poetry,* London, Chatto and Windus, 1961.

Herrnstein, Barbara, ed., *Discussions of Shakespeare's Sonnets,* Boston, Heath, 1964. A very useful collection of essays and excerpts, by various hands.

Hubler, Edward, *The Sense of Shakespeare's Sonnets,* Princeton, Princeton University Press, 1952.

Knight, G. Wilson, *The Mutual Flame,* New York, Macmillan, 1955. On the *Sonnets* and "The Phoenix and Turtle."

Landry, Hilton, *Interpretations in Shakespeare's Sonnets,* Berkeley and Los Angeles, University of California Press, 1963.

Leishman, J. B., *Themes and Variations in Shakespeare's Sonnets,* London, Hutchinson, 1961.

Lever, J. W., *The Elizabethan Love Sonnet,* London, Methuen, 1956.

Lewis, C. S., *English Literature in the Sixteenth Century,* Oxford, Clarendon Press, 1954.

Smith, Hallett, *Elizabethan Poetry,* Cambridge, Mass., Harvard University Press, 1952.

Wilson, J. Dover, *An Introduction to Shakespeare's Sonnets,* Cambridge, Cambridge University Press, 1963.

VENUS AND ADONIS

FIRST EDITION

1593

The Bodleian Copy

VENVS
AND ADONIS

Vilia miretur vulgus: mihi flauus Apollo
Pocula Castalia plena ministret aqua.

LONDON

Imprinted by Richard Field, and are to be sold at
the signe of the white Greyhound in
Paules Church-yard.
1593.

TO THE RIGHT HONORABLE
Henrie VVriothesley, Earle of Southampton,
and Baron of Titchfield.

Ight Honourable, I know not how I shall offend in dedicating my vnpolisht lines to your Lordship, nor how the worlde vvill censure mee for choosing so strong a proppe to support so vveake a burthen, onelye if your Honour seeme but pleased, I account my selfe highly praised, and vowe to take aduantage of all idle houres, till I haue honoured you vvith some grauer labour. But if the first heire of my inuention proue deformed, I shall be sorie it had so noble a god-father : and neuer after eare so barren a land, for feare it yeeld me still so bad a haruest, I leaue it to your Honourable suruey, and your Honor to your hearts content, vvhich I wish may aluvaies ansvvere your ovvne vvish, and the vvorlds hope-full expectation.

Your Honors in all dutie,

William Shakespeare.

VENVS AND ADONIS.

EVEN as the funne with purple-colourd face,
Had tane his laft leaue of the weeping morne,
Rofe-cheekt Adonis hied him to the chace,
Hunting he lou'd, but loue he laught to fcorne:
  Sick-thoughted Venus makes amaine vnto him,
  And like a bold fac'd futer ginnes to woo him.

Thrife fairer then my felfe, (thus fhe began)
The fields chiefe flower, fweet aboue compare,
Staine to all Nimphs, more louely then a man,
More white, and red, then doues, or rofes are:
  Nature that made thee with her felfe at ftrife,
  Saith that the world hath ending with thy life.

Vouchfafe thou wonder to alight thy fteed,
And raine his proud head to the faddle bow,
If thou wilt daine this fauor, for thy meed
A thoufand honie fecrets fhalt thou know:
  Here come and fit, where neuer ferpent hiffes,
  And being fet, Ile fmother thee with kiffes.

B

7

VENVS AND ADONIS.

And yet not cloy thy lips with loth'd facietie,
But rather famifh them amid their plentie,
Making them red, and pale, with frefh varietie:
Ten kiffes fhort as one, one long as twentie:
   A fommers day will feeme an houre but fhort,
   Being wafted in fuch time-beguiling fport.

VVith this fhe ceazeth on his fweating palme,
The prefident of pith, and liuelyhood,
And trembling in her paffion, calls it balme,
Earths foueraigne falue, to do a goddeffe good,
   Being fo enrag'd, defire doth lend her force,
   Couragioufly to plucke him from his horfe.

Ouer one arme the luftie courfers raine,
Vnder her other was the tender boy,
VVho blufht, and powted in a dull difdaine,
VVith leaden appetite, vnapt to toy,
   She red, and hot, as coles of glovving fier,
   He red for fhame, but froftie in defier.

The ftudded bridle on a ragged bough,
Nimbly fhe faftens, (ô how quicke is loue!)
The fteed is ftalled vp, and euen now,
To tie the rider fhe begins to proue:
   Backward fhe pufht him, as fhe would be thruft,
   And gouernd him in ftrength though not in luft.
                         So

VENVS AND ADONIS.

So foone was fhe along, as he was downe,
Each leaning on their elbowes and their hips:
Now doth fhe ftroke his cheek, now doth he frown,
And gins to chide, but foone fhe ftops his lips,
    And kiffing fpeaks, with luftful language broken,
    If thou wilt chide, thy lips fhall neuer open.

He burnes with bafhfull fhame, fhe with her teares
Doth quench the maiden burning of his cheekes,
Then with her windie fighes, and golden heares,
To fan, and blow them drie againe fhe feekes.
    He faith, fhe is immodeft, blames her miffe,
    VVhat followes more, fhe murthers with a kiffe.

Euen as an emptie Eagle fharpe by faft,
Tires with her beake on feathers, flefh, and bone,
Shaking her wings, deuouring all in haft,
Till either gorge be ftuft, or pray be gone:
    Euen fo fhe kift his brow, his cheeke, his chin,
    And where fhe ends, fhe doth anew begin.

Forft to content, but neuer to obey,
Panting he lies, and breatheth in her face.
She feedeth on the fteame, as on a pray,
And calls it heauenly moifture, aire of grace,
    VVifhing her cheeks were gardens ful of flowers,
    So they were dew'd with fuch diftilling fhowers.

B ij

VENVS AND ADONIS.

Looke how a bird lyes tangled in a net,
So faſtned in her armes Adonis lyes,
Pure ſhame and aw'd reſiſtance made him fret,
VVhich bred more beautie in his angrie eyes:
   Raine added to a riuer that is ranke,
   Perforce will force it ouerflow the banke.

Still ſhe intreats, and prettily intreats,
For to a prettie eare ſhe tunes her tale.
Still is he ſullein, ſtill he lowres and frets,
Twixt crimſon ſhame, and anger aſhie pale,
   Being red ſhe loues him beſt, and being white,
   Her beſt is betterd with a more delight.

Looke how he can, ſhe cannot chuſe but loue,
And by her faire immortall hand ſhe ſweares,
From his ſoft boſome neuer to remoue,
Till he take truce with her contending teares,
   VVhich lõg haue raind, making her cheeks al wet,
   And one ſweet kiſſe ſhal pay this comptleſſe debt.

Vpon this promiſe did he raiſe his chin,
Like a diuedapper peering through a waue,
VVho being lookt on, ducks as quickly in:
So offers he to giue what ſhe did craue,
   But when her lips were readie for his pay,
   He winks, and turnes his lips another way.

                     Neuer

VENVS AND ADONIS.

Neuer did paſſenger in ſommers heat,
More thirſt for drinke,then ſhe for this good turne,
Her helpe ſhe ſees,but helpe ſhe cannot get,
She bathes in water, yet her fire muſt burne:
 Oh pitie gan ſhe crie, flint-hearted boy,
 Tis but a kiſſe I begge, why art thou coy?

I haue bene wooed as I intreat thee now,
Euen by the ſterne,and direfull god of warre,
VVhoſe ſinowie necke in battell nere did bow,
VVho conquers where he comes in euerie iarre,
 Yet hath he bene my captiue,and my ſlaue,
 And begd for that which thou vnaskt ſhalt haue.

Ouer my Altars hath he hong his launce,
His battred ſhield, his vncontrolled creſt,
And for my ſake hath learnd to ſport,and daunce,
To toy,to wanton,dallie,ſmile,and ieſt,
 Scorning his churliſh drumme,and enſigne red,
 Making my armes his field, his tent my bed.

Thus he that ouer-ruld, I ouer-ſwayed,
Leading him priſoner in a red roſe chaine,
Strong-temperd ſteele his ſtronger ſtrength obayed.
Yet was he ſeruile to my coy diſdaine,
 Oh be not proud, nor brag not of thy might,
 For maiſtring her that foyld the god of fight.

B iij

VENVS AND ADONIS.

Touch but my lips with thofe faire lips of thine,
Though mine be not fo faire, yet are they red,
The kiffe fhalbe thine owne as well as mine,
VVhat feeft thou in the ground ? hold vp thy head,
    Looke in mine ey-bals, there thy beautie lyes,
    Then why not lips on lips, fince eyes in eyes ?

Art thou afham'd to kiffe ? then winke againe,
And I will winke, fo fhall the day feeme night.
Loue keepes his reuels where there are but twaine:
Be bold to play, our fport is not in fight,
    Thefe blew-veind violets whereon we leane,
    Neuer can blab, nor know not what we meane.

The tender fpring vpon thy tempting lip,
Shewes thee vnripe; yet maift thou well be tafted,
Make vfe of time, let not aduantage flip,
Beautie within it felfe fhould not be wafted,
    Faire flowers that are not gathred in their prime,
    Rot, and confume them felues in litle time.

VVere I hard-fauourd, foule, or wrinckled old,
Il-nurtur'd, crooked, churlifh, harfh in voice,
Ore-worne, defpifed, reumatique, and cold,
Thick-fighted, barren, leane, and lacking iuyce;
    Thē mightft thou paufe, for thē I were not for thee,
    But hauing no defects, why doeft abhor me?

                              Thou

VENVS AND ADONIS.

Thou canſt not ſee one wrinckle in my brow,
Mine eyes are grey, and bright, & quicke in turning:
My beautie as the ſpring doth yearelie grow,
My fleſh is ſoft, and plumpe, my marrow burning,
　My ſmooth moiſt hand, were it with thy hand felt,
　VVould in thy palme diſſolue, or ſeeme to melt.

Bid me diſcourſe, I will inchaunt thine eare,
Or like a Fairie, trip vpon the greene,
Or like a Nimph, with long diſheueled heare,
Daunce on the ſands, and yet no footing ſeene.
　Loue is a ſpirit all compact of fire,
　Not groſſe to ſinke, but light, and will aſpire.

VVitneſſe this Primroſe banke whereon I lie,
Theſe forceleſſe flowers like ſturdy trees ſupport me:
Two ſtrēgthles doues will draw me through the skie,
From morne till night, euen where I liſt to ſport me.
　Is loue ſo light ſweet boy, and may it be,
　That thou ſhould thinke it heauie vnto thee?

Is thine owne heart to thine owne face affected?
Can thy right hand ceaze loue vpon thy left?
Then woo thy ſelfe, be of thy ſelfe reiected:
Steale thine own freedome, and complaine on theft.
　Narciſſus ſo him ſelfe him ſelfe forſooke,
　And died to kiſſe his ſhadow in the brooke.

VENVS AND ADONIS.

Torches are made to light, iewels to weare,
Dainties to taſt, freſh beautie for the vſe,
Herbes for their ſmell, and ſappie plants to beare.
Things growing to them ſelues, are growths abuſe,
 Seeds ſpring frō ſeeds,& beauty breedeth beauty,
 Thou waſt begot, to get it is thy duty.

Vpon the earths increaſe why ſhouldſt thou feed,
Vnleſſe the earth with thy increaſe be fed?
By law of nature thou art bound to breed,
That thine may liue,when thou thy ſelfe art dead:
 And ſo in ſpite of death thou doeſt ſuruiue,
 In that thy likeneſſe ſtill is left aliue.

By this the loue-ſicke Queene began to ſweate,
For where they lay the ſhadow had forſooke them,
And Titan tired in the midday heate,
VVith burning eye did hotly ouer-looke them,
 VViſhing Adonis had his teame to guide,
 So he were like him, and by Venus ſide.

And now Adonis with a lazie ſprite,
And with a heauie, darke, diſliking eye,
His lowring browes ore-whelming his faire ſight,
Like miſtie vapors when they blot the skie,
 So wring his cheekes ,cries,fie, no more of loue,
 The ſunne doth burne my face I muſt remoue.
          Ay,me,

14

VENVS AND ADONIS.

Ay, me, (quoth Venus) young, and so vnkinde,
VVhat bare excuses mak'ft thou to be gon ?
Ile figh celeftiall breath, whofe gentle winde,
Shall coole the heate of this defcending fun:
    Ile make a fhadow for thee of my heares,
    If they burn too,lle quench them with my teares.

The fun that fhines from heauen , fhines but warme,
And lo I lye betweene that funne ,and thee :
The heate I haue from thence doth litle harme,
Thine eye darts forth the fire that burneth me,
    And were I not immortall, life were done,
    Betweene this heauenly,and earthly funne.

Art thou obdurate, flintie, hard as fteele ?
Nay more then flint, for ftone at raine relenteth :
Art thou a womans fonne and canft not feele
VVhat tis to loue, how want of loue tormenteth?
    O had thy mother borne fo hard a minde,
    She had not brought forth thee, but died vnkind.

VVhat am I that thou fhouldft contemne me this ?
Or what great danger, dwels vpon my fute ?
VVhat were thy lips the worfe for one poore kis ?
Speake faire,but fpeake faire words,or elfe be mute:
    Giue me one kiffe, Ile giue it thee againe,
    And one for intreft, if thou wilt haue twaine.

             C

VENVS AND ADONIS.

Fie, liuelesse picture, cold, and sencelesse stone,
VVell painted idoll, image dull, and dead,
Statüe contenting but the eye alone,
Thing like a man, but of no woman bred:
 Thou art no man, though of a mans complexion,
 For men will kisse euen by their owne direction.

This said, impatience chokes her pleading tongue,
And swelling passion doth prouoke a pause,
Red cheeks, and fierie eyes blaze forth her wrong:
Being Iudge in loue, she cannot right her cause.
 And now she weeps, & now she faine would speake
 And now her sobs do her intendments breake.

Sometime she shakes her head, and then his hand,
Now gazeth she on him, now on the ground;
Sometime her armes infold him like a band,
She would, he will not in her armes be bound:
 And when from thence he struggles to be gone,
 She locks her lillie fingers one in one.

Fondling, she saith, since I haue hemd thee here
VVithin the circuit of this iuorie pale,
Ile be a parke, and thou shalt be my deare:
Feed where thou wilt, on mountaine, or in dale;
 Graze on my lips, and if those hils be drie,
 Stray lower, where the pleasant fountaines lie.
        VVi hin

16

VENVS AND ADONIS.

VVitin this limit is reliefe inough,
Sweet bottome graffe, and high delightfull plaine,
Round rifing hillocks, brakes obfcure, and rough,
To fhelter thee from tempeft, and from raine:
    Then be my deare, fince I am fuch a parke,
    No dog fhal rowze thee, though a thoufand bark.

At this Adonis fmiles as in difdaine,
That in ech cheeke appeares a prettie dimple;
Loue made thofe hollowes, if him felfe were flaine,
He might be buried in a tombe fo fimple,
    Foreknowing well, if there he came to lie,
    VVhy there loue liu'd, & there he could not die.

Thefe louely caues, thefe round inchanting pits,
Opend their mouthes to fwallow Venus liking:
Being mad before, how doth fhe now for wits?
Strucke dead at firft, what needs a fecond ftriking?
    Poore Queene of loue, in thine own law forlorne,
    To loue a cheeke that fmiles at thee in fcorne.

Now which way fhall fhe turne? what fhall fhe fay?
Her words are done, her woes the more increafing,
The time is fpent, her obiect will away,
And from her twining armes doth vrge releafing:
    Pitie fhe cries, fome fauour, fome remorfe,
    Away he fprings, and hafteth to his horfe.

                    C ij

17

VENVS AND ADONIS.

But lo from forth a copp's that neighbors by,
A breeding Iennet, luſtie, young, and proud,
Adonis trampling Courſer doth eſpy:
And forth ſhe ruſhes, ſnorts, and neighs aloud.
   The ſtrong-neckt ſteed being tied vnto a tree,
   Breaketh his raine, and to her ſtraight goes hee.

Imperiouſly he leaps, he neighs, he bounds,
And now his wouen girthes he breaks aſunder,
The bearing earth with his hard hoofe he wounds,
VVhoſe hollow wombe reſounds like heauens thun-
   The yron bit he cruſheth tweene his teeth, (der,
   Controlling what he was controlled with.

His eares vp prickt, his braided hanging mane
Vpon his compaſt creſt now ſtand on end,
His noſtrils drinke the aire, and forth againe
As from a fornace, vapors doth he ſend:
   His eye which ſcornfully gliſters like fire,
   Shewes his hote courage, and his high deſire.

Sometime he trots, as if he told the ſteps,
VVith gentle maieſtie, and modeſt pride,
Anon he reres vpright, curuets, and leaps,
As who ſhould ſay, lo thus my ſtrength is tride.
   And this I do, to captiuate the eye,
   Of the faire breeder that is ſtanding by.

                    VVhat

VENVS AND ADONIS.

VVhat recketh he his riders angrie fturre,
His flattering holla, or his ftand, I fay,
VVhat cares he now, for curbe, or pricking fpurre,
For rich caparifons, or trappings gay :
 He fees his loue, and nothing elfe he fees,
 For nothing elfe with his proud fight agrees.

Looke when a Painter would furpaffe the life,
In limming out a well proportioned fteed,
His Art with Natures workmanfhip at ftrife,
As if the dead the liuing fhould exceed :
 So did this Horfe excell a common one,
 In fhape, in courage, colour, pace and bone.

Round hooft, fhort ioynted, fetlocks fhag, and long,
Broad breaft, full eye, fmall head, and noftrill wide,
High creft, fhort eares, ftraight legs, & paffing ftrõg,
Thin mane, thicke taile, broad buttock, tender hide:
 Looke what a Horfe fhould haue, he did not lack,
 Saue a proud rider on fo proud a back.

Sometime he fcuds farre off, aud there he ftares,
Anon he ftarts, at fturring of a feather:
To bid the wind a bafe he now prepares,
And where he runne, or flie, they know not whether:
 For through his mane & taile, the high wind fings,
 Fanning the haires, who waue like feathred wings.

C iij

VENVS AND ADONIS.

He lookes vpon his loue, and neighes vnto her,
She anſwers him, as if ſhe knew his minde,
Being proud as females are, to ſee him woo her,
She puts on outward ſtrangeneſſe, ſeemes vnkinde:
   Spurnes at his loue, and ſcorns the heat he feeles,
   Beating his kind imbracements with her heeles.

Then like a melancholy malcontent,
He vailes his taile that like a falling plume,
Coole ſhadow to his melting buttocke lent,
He ſtamps, and bites the poore flies in his fume :
   His loue perceiuing how he was inrag'd,
   Grew kinder, and his furie was aſſwag'd.

His teſtie maiſter goeth about to take him,
VVhen lo the vnbackt breeder full of feare,
Iealous of catching, ſwiftly doth forſake him,
VVith her the Horſe, and left Adonis there :
   As they were mad vnto the wood they hie them,
   Out ſtripping crowes, that ſtriue to ouerfly them.

All ſwolne with chafing, downe Adonis ſits,
Banning his boyſtrous, and vnruly beaſt;
And now the happie ſeaſon once more fits
That loueſicke loue, by pleading may be bleſt :
   For louers ſay, the heart hath treble wrong,
   VVhen it is bard the aydance of the tongue.

                    An

VENVS AND ADONIS.

An Ouen that is ſtopt, or riuer ſtayd,
Burneth more hotly, ſwelleth with more rage:
So of concealed ſorow may be ſayd,
Free vent of words loues fier doth aſſwage,
   But when the hearts atturney once is mute,
   The client breakes, as deſperat in his ſute.

He ſees her comming, and begins to glow:
Euen as a dying coale reuiues with winde,
And with his bonnet hides his angrie brow,
Lookes on the dull earth with diſturbed minde:
   Taking no notice that ſhe is ſo nye,
   For all askance he holds her in his eye.

O what a ſight it was wiſtly to view,
How ſhe came ſtealing to the wayward boy,
To note the fighting conflict of her hew,
How white and red, ech other did deſtroy:
   But now her cheeke was pale, and by and by
   It flaſht forth fire, as lightning from the skie.

Now was ſhe iuſt before him as he ſat,
And like a lowly louer downe ſhe kneeles,
VVith one faire hand ſhe heaueth vp his hat,
Her other tender hand his faire cheeke feeles:
   His tendrer cheeke, receiues her ſoft hands print,
   As apt, as new falne ſnow takes any dint.

VENVS AND ADONIS.

Oh what a war of lookes was then betweene them,
Her eyes petitioners to his eyes suing,
His eyes saw her eyes, as they had not seene them,
Her eyes wooed still, his eyes disdaind the wooing:
  And all this dumbe play had his acts made plain,
  VVith tears which Chorus-like her eyes did rain.

Full gently now she takes him by the hand,
A lillie prisond in a gaile of snow,
Or Iuorie in an allablaster band,
So white a friend, ingirts so white a fo :
  This beautious combat wilfull, and vnwilling,
  Showed like two siluer doues that sit a billing.

Once more the engin of her thoughts began,
O fairest mouer on this mortall round,
VVould thou wert as I am, and I a man,
My heart all whole as thine, thy heart my wound,
  For one sweet looke thy helpe I would assure thee,
  Thogh nothing but my bodies bane wold cure thee

Giue me my hand (saith he,) why dost thou feele it ?
Giue me my heart (saith she,) and thou shalt haue it.
O giue it me lest thy hard heart do steele it,
And being steeld, soft sighes can neuer graue it.
  Then loues deepe grones, I neuer shall regard,
  Becaufe Adonis heart hath made mine hard.

For

VENVS AND ADONIS.

For fhame he cries, let go, and let me go,
My dayes delight is paft, my horfe is gone,
And tis your fault I am bereft him fo,
I pray you hence, and leaue me here alone,
    For all my mind, my thought, my bufie care,
    Is how to get my palfrey from the mare.

Thus fhe replies, thy palfrey as he fhould,
VVelcomes the warme approch of fweet defire,
Affection is a coale that muft be coold,
Elfe fufferd it will fet the heart on fire,
    The fea hath bounds, but deepe defire hath none,
    Therfore no maruell though thy horfe be gone.

How like a iade he ftood tied to the tree,
Seruilly maifterd with a leatherne raine,
Bnt when he faw his loue, his youths faire fee,
He held fuch pettie bondage in difdaine :
    Throwing the bafe thong from his bending creft,
    Enfranchifing his mouth, his backe, his breft.

VVho fees his true-loue in her naked bed,
Teaching the fheets a whiter hew then white,
But when his glutton eye fo full hath fed,
His other agents ayme at like delight ?
    VVho is fo faint that dares not be fo bold,
    To touch the fier the weather being cold ?

        D

VENVS AND ADONIS.

Let me excuse thy courfer gentle boy,
And learne of him I heartily befeech thee,
To take aduantage on prefented ioy,
Though I were dūbe,yet his proceedings teach thee
O learne to loue, the leffon is but plaine,
And once made perfeƈt, neuer loft againe.

I know not loue (quoth he) nor will not know it,
Vnleffe it be a Boare,and then I chafe it,
Tis much to borrow, and I will not owe it,
My loue to loue, is loue, but to difgrace it,
For I haue heard, it is a life in death,
That laughs and weeps, and all but with a breath.

VVho weares a garment fhapeleffe and vnfinifht?
VVho plucks the bud before one leafe put forth ?
If fpringing things be anie iot diminifht,
They wither in their prime, proue nothing worth,
The colt that's backt and burthend being yong,
Lofeth his pride, and neuer waxeth ftrong.

You hurt my hand with wringing, let vs part,
And leaue this idle theame, this bootleffe chat,
Remoue your fiege from my vnyeelding hart,
To loues allarmes it will not ope the gate,
Difmiffe your vows, your fained tears, your flattry,
For where a heart is hard they make no battry.

what

24

VENVS AND ADONIS.

VVhat canſt thou talke (quoth ſhe) haſt thou a tong?
O would thou hadſt not, or I had no hearing,
Thy marmaides voice hath done me double wrong,
I had my lode before, now preſt with bearing,
  Mellodious diſcord, heauenly tune harſh ſounding,
  Eares deep ſweet muſik, & harts deep ſore wouding

Had I no eyes but eares, my eares would loue,
That inward beautie and inuiſible,
Or were I deafe, thy outward parts would moue
Ech part in me, that were but ſenſible,
  Though neither eyes, nor eares, to heare nor ſee,
  Yet ſhould I be in loue, by touching thee.

Say that the ſence of feeling were bereft me,
And that I could not ſee, nor heare, nor touch,
And nothing but the verie ſmell were left me,
Yet would my loue to thee be ſtill as much,
  For frõ the ſtillitorie of thy face excelling,   (ling.
  Coms breath perfumd, that breedeth loue by ſmel-

But oh what banquet wert thou to the taſt,
Being nourſe, and feeder of the other foure,
VVould they not wiſh the feaſt might euer laſt,
And bid ſuſpition double locke the dore,
  Leſt iealouſie that ſower vnwelcome gueſt,
  Should by his ſtealing in diſturbe the feaſt?

D ij

25

VENVS AND ADONIS.

Once more the rubi-colourd portall opend,
VVhich to his speech did honie paſſage yeeld,
Like a red morne that euer yet betokend,
vvracke to the ſea-man, tempeſt to the field:
   Sorrow to ſhepherds, wo vnto the birds,
    Guſts, and foule flawes, to heardmen, & to herds.

This ill preſage aduiſedly ſhe marketh,
Euen as the wind is huſht before it raineth:
Or as the wolfe doth grin before he barketh:
Or as the berrie breakes before it ſtaineth:
   Or like the deadly bullet of a gun:
    His meaning ſtrucke her ere his words begun.

And at his looke ſhe flatly falleth downe,
For lookes kill loue, and loue by lookes reuiueth,
A ſmile recures the wounding of a frowne,
But bleſſed bankrout that by loue ſo thriueth.
   The ſillie boy beleeuing ſhe is dead,
    Claps her pale cheeke, till clapping makes it red.

And all amaz'd, brake off his late intent,
For ſharply he did thinke to reprehend her,
VVhich cunning loue did wittily preuent,
Faire-fall the wit that can ſo well defend her:
   For on the graſſe ſhe lyes as ſhe were ſlaine,
    Till his breath breatheth life in her againe.

                              He

VENVS AND ADONIS.

He wrings her nose, he strikes her on the cheekes,
He bends her fingers, holds her pulses hard,
He chafes her lips, a thousand wayes he seekes,
To mend the hurt, that his vnkindnesse mard,
　He kisses her, and she by her good will,
　VVill neuer rise, so he will kisse her still.

The night of sorrow now is turnd to day,
Her two blew windowes faintly she vpheaueth,
Like the faire sunne when in his fresh array,
He cheeres the morne, and all the earth releeueth:
　And as the bright sunne glorifies the skie:
　So is her face illumind with her eye.

VVhose beames vpon his hairelesse face are fixt,
As if from thence they borrowed all their shine,
VVere neuer foure such lamps, together mixt,
Had not his clouded with his browes repine:
　But hers, which through the cristal tears gaue light,
　Shone like the Moone in water seene by night.

O where am I (quoth she,) in earth or heauen,
Or in the Ocean drencht, or in the fire:
VVhat houre is this, or morne, or wearie euen,
Do I delight to die or life desire?
　But how I liu'd, and life was deaths annoy,
　But now I dy'de, and death was liuely ioy.

D iij

VENVS AND ADONIS.

O thou didſt kill me, kill me once againe,
Thy eyes ſhrowd tutor, that hard heart of thine,
Hath taught them ſcornfull tricks, & ſuch diſdaine,
That they haue murdred this poore heart of mine,
    And theſe mine eyes true leaders to their queene,
    But for thy piteous lips no more had ſeene.

Long may they kiſſe ech other for this cure,
Oh neuer let their crimſon liueries weare,
And as they laſt, their verdour ſtill endure,
To driue infection from the dangerous yeare :
    That the ſtar-gazers hauing writ on death,
    May ſay, the plague is baniſht by thy breath.

Pure lips, ſweet ſeales in my ſoft lips imprinted,
VVhat bargaines may I make ſtill to be ſealing?
To ſell my ſelfe I can be well contented,
So thou wilt buy, and pay, and vſe good dealing,
    VVhich purchaſe if thou make, for feare of ſlips,
    Set thy ſeale manuell, on my wax-red lips.

A thouſand kiſſes buyes my heart from me,
And pay them at thy leiſure, one by one,
VVhat is ten hundred touches vnto thee,
Are they not quickly told, and quickly gone ?
    Say for non-paimēt, that the debt ſhould double,
    Is twentie hundred kiſſes ſuch a trouble ?

                         Faire

VENVS AND ADONIS.

Faire Queene (quoth he) if anie loue you owe me,
Measure my strangenesse with my vnripe yeares,
Before I know my selfe, seeke not to know me,
No fisher but the vngrowne frie forbeares,
  The mellow plum doth fall, the greene sticks fast,
  Or being early pluckt, is sower to taste.

Looke the worlds comforter with wearie gate,
His dayes hot taske hath ended in the west,
The owle (nights herald) shreeks, tis verie late,
The sheepe are gone to fold, birds to their nest,
  And cole-black clouds, that shadow heauens light,
  Do summon vs to part, and bid good night.

Now let me say goodnight, and so say you,
If you will say so, you shall haue a kis;
Goodnight (quoth she) and ere he sayes adue,
The honie fee of parting tendred is,
  Her armes do lend his necke a sweet imbrace,
  Incorporate then they seeme, face growes to face.

Till breathlesse he disioynd, and backward drew,
The heauenly moisture that sweet corall mouth,
VVhose precious tast, her thirstie lips well knew,
VVhereon they surfet, yet complaine on drouth,
  He with her plentie prest, she faint with dearth,
  Their lips together glewed, fall to the earth.

VENVS AND ADONIS.

Now quicke desire hath caught the yeelding pray,
And gluttonlike she feeds, yet neuer filleth,
Her lips are conquerers, his lips obay,
Paying what ransome the insulter willeth :
  VVhose vultur thought doth pitch the price so hie,
  That she will draw his lips rich treasure drie.

And hauing felt the sweetnesse of the spoile,
VVith blind fold furie she begins to forrage,
Her face doth reeke,& smoke,her blood doth boile,
And carelesse lust stirs vp a desperat courage,
  Planting obliuion, beating reason backe,
  Forgetting shames pure blush,& honors wracke.

Hot, faint, and wearie, with her hard imbracing,
Like a wild bird being tam'd with too much hādling,
Or as the fleet-foot Roe that's tyr'd with chasing,
Or like the froward infant stild with dandling:
  He now obayes, and now no more resisteth,
  VVhile she takes all she can, not all she listeth.

VVhat waxe so frozen but dissolues with tempring,
And yeelds at last to euerie light impression ?
Things out of hope, are compast oft with ventring,
Chiefly in loue, whose leaue exceeds commission :
  Affection faints not like a pale-fac'd coward,
  But the woes best, whē most his choice is froward.
                              vvhen

VENVS AND ADONIS.

VVhen he did frowne,ô had she then gaue ouer,
Such nectar from his lips she had not suckt,
Foule wordes,and frownes,must not repell a louer,
VVhat though the rose haue prickles, yet tis pluckt?
　VVere beautie vnder twentie locks kept fast,
　　Yet loue breaks through,& picks them all at last.

For pittie now she can no more detaine him,
The poore foole praies her that he may depart,
She is resolu'd no longer to restraine him,
Bids him farewell,and looke well to her hart,
　The which by Cupids bow she doth protest,
　　He carries thence incaged in his brest.

Sweet boy she saies,this night ile wast in sorrow,
For my sick heart commands mine eyes to watch,
Tell me loues maister,shall we meete to morrow,
Say, shall we, shall we, wilt thou make the match?
　He tell's her no,to morrow he intends,
　　To hunt the boare with certaine of his frends.

The boare (quoth she) whereat a suddain pale,
Like lawne being spred vpon the blushing rose,
Vsurpes her cheeke,she trembles at his tale,
And on his neck her yoaking armes she throwes.
　She sincketh downe,still hanging by his necke,
　　He on her belly fall's,she on her backe.

　　　　　　　E

31

VENVS AND ADONIS.

Now is she in the verie lifts of loue,
Her champion mounted for the hot incounter,
All is imaginarie she doth proue,
He will not mannage her, although he mount her,
    That worse then Tantalus is her annoy,
    To clip Elizium, and to lacke her ioy.

Euen so poore birds deceiu'd with painted grapes,
Do surfet by the eye, and pine the maw :
Euen so she languisheth in her mishaps,
As those poore birds that helplesse berries saw,
    The warme effects which she in him finds missing,
    She seekes to kindle with continuall kissing.

But all in vaine, good Queene, it will not bee,
She hath assai'd as much as may be prou'd,
Her pleading hath deseru'd a greater fee,
She's loue; she loues, and yet she is not lou'd,
    Fie, fie, he saies, you crush me, let me go,
    You haue no reason to withhold me so.

Thou hadst bin gone (quoth she) sweet boy ere this,
But that thou toldst me, thou woldst hunt the boare,
Oh be aduisd, thou know'st not what it is,
VVith iauelings point a churlish swine to goare,
    VVhose tushes neuer sheathd, he whetteth still,
    Like to a mortall butcher bent to kill.

                              On

VENVS AND ADONIS.

On his bow-backe, he hath a battell set,
Of brisly pikes that euer threat his foes,
His eyes like glow-wormes shine,when he doth fret
His snout digs sepulchers where ere he goes,
 Being mou'd he strikes, what ere is in his way,
 And whom he strikes, his crooked tushes slay.

His brawnie sides with hairie bristles armed,
Are better proofe then thy speares point can enter,
His short thick necke cannot be easily harmed,
Being irefull,on the lyon he will venter,
 The thornie brambles,and imbracing bushes,
 As fearefull of him part,through whom he rushes.

Alas,he naught esteem's that face of thine,
To which loues eyes paies tributarie gazes,
Nor thy soft handes,sweet lips,and christall eine,
VVhose full perfection all the world amazes,
 But hauing thee at vantage(wondrous dread!)
 VVold roote these beauties,as he root's the mead.

Oh let him keep his loathsome cabin still,
Beautie hath nanght to do with such foule fiends,
Come not within his danger by thy will,
They that thriue well,take counsell of their friends,
 VVhen thou didst name the boare,not to disseble,
 I feard thy fortune,aud my ioynts did tremble.
E ij

VENVS AND ADONIS.

Didſt thou not marke my face, was it not white?
Saweſt thou not ſignes of feare lurke in mine eye?
Grew I not faint, and fell I not downe right?
VVithin my boſome whereon thou doeſt lye,
    My boding heart, pants, beats, and takes no reſt,
    But like an earthquake, ſhakes thee on my breſt.

For where loue raignes, diſturbing iealouſie,
Doth call him ſelfe affections centinell,
Giues falſe alarmes, ſuggeſteth mutinie,
And in a peacefull houre doth crie, kill, kill,
    Diſtempring gentle loue in his deſire,
    As aire, and water do abate the fire.

This ſower informer, this bate-breeding ſpie,
This canker that eates vp loues tender ſpring,
This carry-tale, diſſentious iealouſie,
That ſomtime true newes, ſomtime falſe doth bring,
    Knocks at my heart, and whiſpers in mine eare,
    That if I loue thee, I thy death ſhould feare.

And more then ſo, preſenteth to mine eye,
The picture of an angrie chafing boare,
Vnder whoſe ſharpe fangs, on his backe doth lye,
An image like thy ſelfe, all ſtaynd with goare,
    vvhoſe blood vpon the freſh flowers being ſhed,
    Doth make thē droop with grief, & hang the hed.
                                                    what

34

VENVS AND ADONIS.

VVhat should I do, seeing thee so indeed?
That tremble at th'imagination,
The thought of it doth make my faint heart bleed,
And feare doth teach it diuination;
    I prophecie thy death, my liuing sorrow,
    If thou incounter with the boare to morrow.

But if thou needs wilt hunt, be rul'd by me,
Vncouple at the timerous flying hare,
Or at the foxe which liues by subtiltie,
Or at the Roe which no incounter dare:
    Pursue these fearfull creatures o're the downes,
    And on thy wel breathd horse keep with thy houds

And when thou hast on foote the purblind hare,
Marke the poore wretch to ouer-shut his troubles,
How he outruns the wind, and with what care,
He crankes and crosses with a thousand doubles,
    The many musits through the which he goes,
    Are like a laberinth to amaze his foes.

Sometime he runnes among a flocke of sheepe,
To make the cunning hounds mistake their smell,
And sometime where earth-deluing Conies keepe,
To stop the loud pursuers in their yell:
    And sometime sorteth with a heard of deare,
    Danger deuiseth shifts, wit waites on feare.

E iij

VENVS AND ADONIS.

For there his fmell with others being mingled,
The hot fent-fnuffing hounds are driuen to doubt,
Ceafing their clamorous cry, till they haue fingled
VVith much ado the cold fault cleanly out,
 Then do they fpend their mouth's, eccho replies,
 As if an other chafe were in the skies.

By this poore wat farre off vpon a hill,
Stands on his hinder-legs with liftning eare,
To hearken if his foes purfue him ftill,
Anon their loud alarums he doth heare,
 And now his griefe may be compared well,
 To one fore ficke, that heares the paffing bell.

Then fhalt thou fee the deaw-bedabbled wretch,
Turne, and returne, indenting with the way,
Ech enuious brier, his wearie legs do fcratch,
Ech fhadow makes him ftop, ech murmour ftay,
 For miferie is troden on by manie,
 And being low, neuer releeu'd by anie.

Lye quietly, and heare a litle more,
Nay do not ftruggle, for thou fhalt not rife,
To make thee hate the hunting of the bore,
Vnlike my felfe thou hear'ft me moralize,
 Applying this to that, and fo to fo,
 For loue can comment vpon euerie wo.

VVhere

36

VENVS AND ADONIS.

VVhere did I leaue? no matter where(quoth he)
Leaue me, and then the ftorie aptly ends,
The night is fpent; why what of that (quoth fhe?)
I am (quoth he) expected of my friends,
   And now tis darke, and going I fhall fall.
   In night (quoth fhe) defire fees beft of all.

But if thou fall, oh then imagine this,
The earth in loue with thee, thy footing trips,
And all is but to rob thee of a kis,
Rich prayes make true-men theeues: fo do thy lips
   Make modeft Dyan, cloudie and forlorne,
   Left fhe fhould fteale a kiffe and die forfworne.

Now of this darke night I perceiue the reafon,
Cinthia for fhame, obfcures her filuer fhine,
Till forging nature be condemn'd of treafon,
For ftealing moulds from heauen, that were diuine,
   VVherin fhe fram'd thee, in hie heauens defpight,
   To fhame the funne by day, and her by night.

And therefore hath fhe brib'd the deftinies,
To croffe the curious workmanfhip of nature,
To mingle beautie with infirmities,
And pure perfection with impure defeature,
   Making it fubiect to the tyrannie,
   Of mad mifchances, and much miferie.

VENVS AND ADONIS.

As burning feauers, agues pale, and faint,
Life-poyſoning peſtilence, and frendzies wood,
The marrow-eating ſickneſſe whoſe attaint,
Diſorder breeds by heating of the blood,
    Surfets, impoſtumes, griefe, and damnd diſpaire,
    Sweare natures death, for framing thee ſo faire.

And not the leaſt of all theſe maladies,
But in one minutes fight brings beautie vnder,
Both fauour, ſauour, hew, and qualities,
VVhereat the th'impartiall gazer late did wonder,
    Are on the ſudden waſted, thawed, and donne,
    As mountain ſnow melts with the midday ſonne.

Therefore deſpight of fruitleſſe chaſtitie,
Loue-lacking veſtals, and ſelfe-louing Nuns,
That on the earth would breed a ſcarcitie,
And barraine dearth of daughters, and of ſuns;
    Be prodigall, the lampe that burnes by night,
    Dries vp his oyle, to lend the world his light.

VVhat is thy bodie but a ſwallowing graue,
Seeming to burie that poſteritie,
VVhich by the rights of time thou needs muſt haue,
If thou deſtroy them not in darke obſcuritie?
    If ſo the world will hold thee in diſdaine,
    Sith in thy pride, ſo faire a hope is ſlaine.

                         So

VENVS AND ADONIS.

So in thy selfe, thy selfe art made away,
A mischiefe worse then ciuill home-bred strife,
Or theirs whose desperat hands them selues do slay,
Or butcher sire, that reaues his sonne of life:
  Foule cankring rust, the hidden treasure frets,
  But gold that's put to vse more gold begets.

Nay then (quoth Adon) you will fall againe,
Into your idle ouer-handled theame,
The kisse I gaue you is bestow'd in vaine,
And all in vaine you striue against the streame,
  For by this black-fac't night, desires foule nourse,
  Your treatise makes me like you, worse & worse.

If loue haue lent you twentie thousand tongues,
And euerie tongue more mouing then your owne,
Bewitching like the wanton Marmaids songs,
Yet from mine eare the tempting tune is blowne,
  For know my heart stands armed in mine eare,
  And will not let a false sound enter there.

Lest the deceiuing harmonie should ronne,
Into the quiet closure of my brest,
And then my litle heart were quite vndone,
In his bed-chamber to be bard of rest,
  No Ladie no, my heart longs not to grone,
  But soundly sleeps, while now it sleeps alone.

F

39

VENVS AND ADONIS.

VVhat haue you vrg'd, that I can not reproue?
The path is smooth that leadeth on to danger,
I hate not loue, but your deuise in loue,
That lends imbracements vnto euery stranger,
    You do it for increase, ô straunge excuse!
    VVhen reason is the bawd to lusts abuse.

Call it not loue, for loue to heauen is fled,
Since sweating lust on earth vsurpt his name,
Vnder whose simple semblance he hath fed,
Vpon fresh beautie, blotting it with blame;
    VVhich the hot tyrant staines,& soone bereaues:
    As Caterpillers do the tender leaues.

Loue comforteth like sun-shine after raine,
But lusts effect is tempest after sunne,
Loues gentle spring doth alwayes fresh remaine,
Lusts winter comes, ere sommer halfe be donne:
    Loue surfets not, lust like a glutton dies:
    Loue is all truth, lust full of forged lies.

More I could tell, but more I dare not say,
The text is old, the Orator too greene,
Therefore in sadnesse, now I will away,
My face is full of shame, my heart of teene,
    Mine eares that to your wanton talke attended,
    Do burne them selues, for hauing so offended.
                    VVith

VENVS AND ADONIS.

VVith this he breaketh from the sweet embrace,
Of those faire armes which bound him to her brest,
And homeward through the dark lawnd runs apace,
Leaues loue vpon her backe, deeply distrest,
    Looke how a bright star shooteth from the skye;
    So glides he in the night from Venus eye.

VVhich after him she dartes, as one on shore
Gazing vpon a late embarked friend,
Till the wilde waues will haue him seene no more,
VVhose ridges with the meeting cloudes contend:
    So did the mercilesse, and pitchie night,
    Fold in the obiect that did feed her sight.

VVhereat amasd as one that ynaware,
Hath dropt a precious iewell in the flood,
Or stonisht, as night wandrers often are,
Their light blowne out in some mistrustfull wood;
    Euen so confounded in the darke she lay,
    Hauing lost the faire discouerie of her way.

And now she beates her heart, whereat it grones,
That all the neighbour caues as seeming troubled,
Make verball repetition of her mones,
Passion on passion, deeply is redoubled,
    Ay me, she cries, and twentie times, wo, wo,
    And twentie ecchoes, twentie times crie so,

VENVS AND ADONIS.

She marking them, begins a wailing note,
And sings extemporally a wofull dittie,
How loue makes yong-men thrall, & old men dote,
How loue is wise in follie, foolish wittie:
  Her heauie antheme still concludes in wo,
  And still the quier of ecchoes answer so.

Her song was tedious, and out-wore the night,
For louers houres are long, though seeming short,
If pleasd themselues, others they thinke delight,
In such like circumstance, with such like sport:
  Their copious stories oftentimes begunne,
  End without audience, and are neuer donne.

For who hath she to spend the night withall,
But idle sounds resembling parasits?
Like shrill-tongu'd Tapsters answering euerie call,
Soothing the humor of fantastique wits,
  She sayes tis so, they answer all tis so,
  And would say after her, if she said no.

Lo here the gentle larke wearie of rest,
From his moyst cabinet mounts vp on hie,
And wakes the morning, from whose siluer brest,
The sunne ariseth in his maiestie,
  VVho doth the world so glorioufly behold,
  That Ceader tops and hils, seeme burnisht gold.
                    Venus

VENVS AND ADONIS.

Venus falutes him with this faire good morrow,
Oh thou cleare god, and patron of all light,
From whom ech lamp, and fhining ftar doth borrow,
The beautious influence that makes him bright,
    There liues a fonne that fuckt an earthly mother,
    May lend thee light, as thou doeft lend to other.

This fayd, fhe hafteth to a mirtle groue,
Mufing the morning is fo much ore-worne,
And yet fhe heares no tidings of her loue;
She harkens for his hounds, and for his horne,
    Anon fhe heares them chaunt it luftily,
    And all in haft fhe coafteth to the cry.

And as fhe runnes, the bufhes in the way,
Some catch her by the necke, fome kiffe her face,
Some twin'd about her thigh to make her ftay,
She wildly breaketh from their ftrict imbrace,
    Like a milch Doe, whofe fwelling dugs do ake,
    Hafting to feed her fawne, hid in fome brake,

By this fhe heares the hounds are at a bay,
VVhereat fhe ftarts like one that fpies an adder,
VVreath'd vp in fatall folds iuft in his way,
The feare whereof doth make him fhake, & fhudder,
    Euen fo the timerous yelping of the hounds,
    Appals her fenfes, and her fpirit confounds.

F iij

VENVS AND ADONIS.

For now she knowes it is no gentle chase,
But the blunt boare, rough beare, or lyon proud,
Because the crie remaineth in one place,
VVhere fearefully the dogs exclaime aloud,
　　Finding their enemie to be so curst,
　　They all straine curt'sie who shall cope him first.

This dismall crie rings sadly in her eare,
Through which it enters to surprise her hart,
VVho ouercome by doubt, and bloodlesse feare,
VVith cold-pale weakenesse, nums ech feeling part,
　　Like soldiers when their captain once doth yeeld,
　　They basely flie, and dare not stay the field.

Thus stands she in a trembling extasie,
Till cheering vp her senses all dismayd,
She tels them tis a causlesse fantasie,
And childish error that they are affrayd,
　　Bids thē leaue quaking, bids them feare no more,
　　And with that word, she spide the hunted boare.

VVhose frothie mouth bepainted all with red,
Like milke, & blood, being mingled both togither,
A second feare through all her sinewes spred,
VVhich madly hurries her, she knowes not whither,
　　This way she runs, and now she will no further,
　　But backe retires, to rate the boare for murther.

A

VENVS AND ADONIS.

A thousand spleenes beare her a thousand wayes,
She treads the path, that she vntreads againe;
Her more then hast, is mated with delayes,
Like the proceedings of a drunken braine,
　　Full of respects, yet naught at all respecting,
　　In hand with all things, naught at all effecting.

Here kenneld in a brake, she finds a hound,
And askes the wearie caitiffe for his maister,
And there another licking of his wound,
Gainst venimd sores, the onely soueraigne plaister.
　　And here she meets another, sadly skowling,
　　To whom she speaks, & he replies with howling.

VVhen he hath ceast his ill resounding noise,
Another flapmouthd mourner, blacke, and grim,
Against the welkin, volies out his voyce,
Another, and another, answer him,
　　Clapping their proud tailes to the ground below,
　　Shaking their scratcht-eares, bleeding as they go.

Looke how, the worlds poore people are amazed,
At apparitions, signes, and prodigies,
VVhereon with feareful eyes, they long haue gazed,
Infusing them with dreadfull prophecies;
　　So she at these sad signes, drawes vp her breath,
　　And sighing it againe, exclaimes on death.

VENVS AND ADONIS.

Hard fauourd tyrant, ougly, meagre, leane,
Hatefull diuorce of loue, (thus chides fhe death)
Grim-grinning ghoſt, earths-worme what doſt thou
To ſtifle beautie, and to ſteale his breath? (meane?
 VVho when he liu'd, his breath and beautie ſet
 Gloſſe on the roſe, ſmell to the violet.

If he be dead, ô no, it cannot be,
Seeing his beautie, thou ſhouldſt ſtrike at it,
Oh yes, it may, thou haſt no eyes to ſee,
But hatefully at randon doeſt thou hit,
 Thy marke is feeble age, but thy falſe dart,
 Miſtakes that aime, and cleaues an infants hart.

Hadſt thou but bid beware, then he had ſpoke,
And hearing him, thy power had loſt his power,
The deſtinies will curſe thee for this ſtroke,
They bid thee crop a weed, thou pluckſt a flower,
 Loues golden arrow at him ſhould haue fled,
 And not deaths ebon dart to ſtrike him dead.

Doſt thou drink tears, that thou prouok'ſt ſuch wee-
VVhat may a heauie grone aduantage thee? (ping,
VVhy haſt thou caſt into eternall ſleeping,
Thoſe eyes that taught all other eyes to ſee?
 Now nature cares not for thy mortall vigour,
 Since her beſt worke is ruin'd with thy rigour.

           Here

46

VENVS AND ADONIS.

Here ouercome as one full of difpaire,
She vaild her eye-lids, who like fluces ftopt
The chriftall tide, that from her two cheeks faire,
In the fweet channell of her bofome dropt.
But through the floud-gates breaks the filuer rain,
And with his ftrong courfe opens them againe.

O how her eyes, and teares, did lend, and borrow,
Her eye feene in the teares, teares in her eye,
Both chriftals, where they viewd ech others forrow:
Sorrow, that friendly fighs fought ftill to drye,
But like a ftormie day, now wind, now raine,
Sighs drie her cheeks, tears make thē wet againe.

Variable paffions throng her conftant wo,
As ftriuing who fhould beft become her griefe,
All entertaind, ech paffion labours fo,
That euerie prefent forrow feemeth chiefe,
But none is beft, then ioyne they all together,
Like many clouds, confulting for foule weather.

By this farre off, fhe heares fome huntfman hallow,
A nourfes fong nere pleafd her babe fo well,
The dyre imagination fhe did follow,
This found of hope doth labour to expell,
For now reuiuing ioy bids her reioyce,
And flatters her, it is Adonis voyce.

G

47

VENVS AND ADONIS.

VVhereat her teares began to turne their tide,
Being prifond in her eye:like pearles in glaffe,
Yet fometimes fals an orient drop befide,
VVhich her cheeke melts,as fcorning it fhould paffe
   To wafh the foule face of the fluttifh ground,
    VVho is but dronken when fhe feemeth drownd.

O hard beleeuing loue how ftrange it feemes!
Not to beleeue,and yet too credulous:
Thy weale,and wo,are both of them extreames,
Defpaire,and hope,makes thee ridiculous.
   The one doth flatter thee in thoughts vnlikely,
    In likely thoughts the other kils thee quickly.

Now fhe vnweaues the web that fhe hath wrought,
Adonis liues, and death is not to blame:
It was not fhe that cald him all to nought;
Now fhe ads honours to his hatefull name.
   She clepes him king of graues,& graue for kings,
    Imperious fupreme of all mortall things.

No,no, quoth fhe, fweet death, I did but ieft,
Yet pardon me, I felt a kind of feare
VVhen as I met the boare,that bloodie beaft,
VVhich knowes no pitie but is ftill feuere,
   Then gentle fhadow(truth I muft confeffe)
    I rayld on thee, fearing my loues deceffe.

                            Tis

VENVS AND ADONIS.

Tis not my fault,the Bore prouok't my tong,
Be wreak't on him (inuifible commaunder)
T'is he foule creature,that hath done thee wrong,
I did but act,he's author of thy flaunder.
    Greefe hath two tongues, and neuer woman yet,
    Could rule them both,without ten womens wit.

Thus hoping that Adonis is aliue,
Her rafh fufpect fhe doth extenuate,
And that his beautie may the better thriue,
VVith death fhe humbly doth infinuate.
    Tels him of trophies,ftatues,tombes,and ftories,
    His victories, his triumphs, and his glories.

O Ioue quoth fhe, how much a foole was I,
To be of fuch a weake and fillie mind,
To waile his death who liues, and muft not die,
Till mutuall ouerthrow of mortall kind ?
    For he being dead, with him is beautie flaine,
    And beautie dead,blacke Chaos comes againe.

Fy, fy, fond loue, thou art as full of feare,
As one with treafure laden,hem'd with theeues,
Trifles vnwitneffed with eye,or eare,
Thy coward heart with falfe bethinking greeues.
    Euen at this word fhe heares a merry horne,
    VVhereat fhe leaps,that was but late forlorne.

G 2

VENVS AND ADONIS.

As Faulcons to the lure, away she flies,
The grasse stoops not, she treads on it so light,
And in her hast, vnfortunately spies,
The foule boares conquest, on her faire delight,
  VVhich seene,her eyes are murdred with the view,
  Like stars asham'd of day, themselues withdrew.

Or as the snaile, whose tender hornes being hit,
Shrinks backward in his shellie caue with paine,
And, there all smoothred vp, in shade doth sit,
Long after fearing to creepe forth againe:
  So at his bloodie view her eyes are fled,
  Into the deep-darke cabbins of her head.

VVhere they resigne their office,and their light,
To the disposing of her troubled braine,
VVho bids them still consort with ougly night,
And neuer wound the heart with lookes againe,
  VVho like a king perplexed in his throne,
  By their suggestion, giues a deadly grone.

VVhereat ech tributarie subiect quakes,
As when the wind imprisond in the ground,
Struggling for passage, earths foundation shakes,
which with cold terror, doth mens minds confound:
  This mutinie ech part doth so surprise,
  That frō their dark beds once more leap her eies.
                     And

VENVS AND ADONIS.

And being opend, threw vnwilling light,
Vpon the wide wound, that the boare had trencht
In his foft flanke, whofe wonted lillie white
VVith purple tears that his wound wept, had drēcht.
  No floure was nigh, no graffe, hearb, leaf, or weed,
  But ftole his blood, and feemd with him to bleed.

This folemne fympathie, poore Venus noteth,
Ouer one fhoulder doth fhe hang her head,
Dumblie fhe paffions, frantikely fhe doteth,
She thinkes he could not die, he is not dead,
  Her voice is ftopt, her ioynts forget to bow,
  Her eyes are mad, that they haue wept till now.

Vpon his hurt fhe lookes fo ftedfaftly,
That her fight dazling, makes the wound feem three,
And then fhe reprehends her mangling eye,
That makes more gafhes, where no breach fhuld be:
  His face feems twain, ech feuerall lim is doubled,
  For oft the eye miftakes, the brain being troubled

My tongue cannot expreffe my griefe for one,
And yet (quoth fhe) behold two Adons dead,
My fighes are blowne away, my falt teares gone,
Mine eyes are turn'd to fire, my heart to lead,
  Heauie hearts lead melt at mine eyes red fire,
  So fhall I die by drops of hot defire.
              G iij

VENVS AND ADONIS.

Alas poore world what treasure haft thou loft,
VVhat face remains aliue that's worth the viewing?
VVhose tongue is mufick now?what caſt thou boaſt,
Of things long fince,or any thing infuing?
  The flowers are fweet, their colours freſh,and trim,
  But true fweet beautie liu'd,and di'de with him.

Bonnet,nor vaile henceforth no creature weare,
Nor funne, nor wind will euer ſtriue to kiffe you,
Hauing no faire to lofe,you need not feare,
The fun doth skorne you,& the wind doth hiffe you.
  But when Adonis liu'de,funne,and ſharpe aire,
  Lurkt like two theeues,to rob him of his faire.

And therefore would he put his bonnet on,
Vnder whofe brim the gaudie funne would peepe,
The wind would blow it off,and being gon,
Play with his locks,then would Adonis weepe.
  And ſtraight in pittie of his tender yeares, (teares.
  They both would ſtriue who firſt ſhould drie his

To fee his face the Lion walkt along,
Behind fome hedge,becaufe he would not fear him:
To recreate himfelf when he hath fong,
The Tygre would be tame,and gently heare him.
  If he had fpoke,the wolfe would leaue his praie,
  And neuer fright the fillie lambe that daie.

                        when

VENVS AND ADONIS.

VVhen he beheld his shadow in the brooke,
The fishes spread on it their golden gils,
VVhen he was by the birds such pleasure tooke,
That some would sing,some other in their bils
   VVould bring him mulberries & ripe-red cherries,
   He fed them with his sight,they him with berries.

But this foule,grim,and vrchin-snowted Boare,
VVhose downeward eye still looketh for a graue:
Ne're saw the beautious liuerie that he wore,
VVitnesse the intertainment that he gaue.
   If he did see his face,why then I know,
   He thought to kisse him, and hath kild him so.

Tis true,tis true,thus was Adonis slaine,
He ran vpon the Boare with his sharpe speare,
VVho did not whet his teeth at him againe,
But by a kisse thought to persuade him there.
   And nousling in his flanke the louing swine,
   Sheath'd vnaware the tuske in his soft groine.

Had I bin tooth'd like him I must confesse,
VVith kissing him I should haue kild him first,
But he is dead,and neuer did he blesse
My youth with his, the more am I accurst.
   VVith this she falleth in the place she stood,
   And staines her face with his congealed bloud.

VENVS AND ADONIS.

She lookes vpon his lips, and they are pale,
She takes him by the hand, and that is cold,
She whifpers in his eares a heauie tale,
As if they heard the wofull words fhe told:
   She lifts the coffer-lids that clofe his eyes,
   VVhere lo, two lamps burnt out in darkneffe lies.

Two glaffes where her felfe, her felfe beheld
A thoufand times, and now no more refleƈt,
Their vertue loft, wherein they late exceld,
And euerie beautie robd of his effeƈt;
   VVonder of time(quoth fhe)this is my fpight,
   That thou being dead, the day fhuld yet be light.

Since thou art dead, lo here I prophecie,
Sorrow on loue hereafter fhall attend :
It fhall be wayted on with iealoufie,
Find fweet beginning, but vnfauorie end.
   Nere fetled equally, but high or lo,
   That all loues pleafure fhall not match his wo.

It fhall be fickle, falfe, and full of fraud,
Bud, and be blafted, in a breathing while,
The bottome poyfon, and the top ore-ftrawd
VVith fweets, that fhall the trueft fight beguile,
   The ftrongeft bodie fhall it make moft weake,
   Strike the wife dūbe, & teach the foole to fpeake.

                                       It

VENVS AND ADONIS.

It ſhall be ſparing, and too full of ryot,
Teaching decrepit age to tread the meaſures,
The ſtaring ruffian ſhall it keepe in quiet,
Pluck down the rich, inrich the poore with treaſures,
 It ſhall be raging mad, and ſillie milde,
 Make the yoong old, the old become a childe.

It ſhall ſuſpect where is no cauſe of feare,
It ſhall not feare where it ſhould moſt miſtruſt,
It ſhall be mercifull, and too ſeueare,
And moſt deceiuing, when it ſeemes moſt iuſt,
 Peruerſe it ſhall be, where it ſhowes moſt toward,
 Put feare to valour, courage to the coward.

It ſhall be cauſe of warre, and dire euents,
And ſet diſſention twixt the ſonne, and ſire,
Subiect, and ſeruill to all diſcontents:
As drie combuſtious matter is to fire,
 Sith in his prime, death doth my loue deſtroy,
 They that loue beſt, their loues ſhall not enioy.

By this the boy that by her ſide laie kild,
VVas melted like a vapour from her ſight,
And in his blood that on the ground laie ſpild,
A purple floure ſproong vp, checkred with white,
 Reſembling well his pale cheekes, and the blood,
 VVhich in round drops, vpō their whiteneſſe ſtood.

H

VENVS AND ADONIS.

She bowes her head, the new-sprong floure to smel,
Comparing it to her Adonis breath,
And saies within her bosome it shall dwell,
Since he himselfe is reft from her by death;
    She crop's the stalke, and in the breach appeares,
    Green-dropping sap, which she compares to teares.

Poore floure(quoth she)this was thy fathers guise,
Sweet issue of a more sweet smelling sire,
For euerie little griefe to wet his eies,
To grow vnto himselfe was his desire;
    And so tis thine, but know it is as good,
    To wither in my brest, as in his blood.

Here was thy fathers bed, here in my brest,
Thou art the next of blood, and tis thy right.
Lo in this hollow cradle take thy rest,
My throbbing hart shall rock thee day and night;
    There shall not be one minute in an houre,
    VVherein I wil not kisse my sweet loues floure.

Thus weary of the world, away she hies,
And yokes her siluer doues, by whose swift aide,
Their mistresse mounted through the emptie skies,
In her light chariot, quickly is conuaide,
    Holding their course to Paphos, where their queen,
    Meanes to immure her selfe, and not be seen.
FINIS

LUCRECE

FIRST EDITION

1594

The Elizabethan Club Copy

LVCRECE.

LONDON.

Printed by Richard Field, for Iohn Harrison, and are
to be sold at the signe of the vhite Greyhound
in Paules Churh-yard.   1594.

TO THE RIGHT

HONOVRABLE, HENRY
VVriothesley, Earle of Southhampton,
and Baron of Titchfield.

HE loue I dedicate to your Lordship is without end:wherof this Pamphlet without beginning is but a superfluous Moity. The warrant I haue of your Honourable disposition, not the worth of my vntutord Lines makes it assured of acceptance. VVhat I haue done is yours, what I haue to doe is yours, being part in all I haue, deuoted yours. VVere my worth greater, my duety would shew greater, meane time, as it is, it is bound to your Lordship; To whom I wish long life still lengthned with all happinesse.

Your Lordships in all duety.

William Shakespeare.

A 2

THE ARGVMENT.

LVcius Tarquinius (for his excessiue pride surnamed Superbus) after hee had caused his owne father in law Seruius Tullius to be cruelly murdred, and contrarie to the Romaine lawes and customes, not requiring or staying for the peoples suffrages, had possessed himselfe of the kingdome: went accompanyed with his sonnes and other Noble men of Rome, to besiege Ardea, during which siege, the principall men of the Army meeting one euening at the Tent of Sextus Tarquinius the Kings sonne, in their discourses after supper euery one commended the vertues of his owne wife: among whom Colatinus extolled the incomparable chastity of his wife Lucretia. In that pleasant humor they all posted to Rome, and intending by theyr secret and sodaine arriuall to make triall of that which euery one had before auouched, onely Colatinus finds his wife (though it were late in the night) spinning amongest her maides, the other Ladies were all found dauncing and reuelling, or in seuerall disports: whereupon the Noble men yeelded Colatinus the victory, and his wife the Fame. At that time Sextus Tarquinius being enflamed with Lucrece beauty, yet smoothering his passions for the present, departed with the rest backe to the Campe: from whence he shortly after priuily withdrew himselfe, and was (according to his estate) royally entertayned and lodged by Lucrece at Colatium. The same night he tretcherouslie stealeth into her Chamber, violently rauisht her, and early in the morning speedeth away. Lucrece in this lamentable plight, hastily dispatcheth Messengers, one to Rome for her father, another to the Campe for Colatine. They came, the one accompanyed with Iunius Brutus, the other with Publius Valerius: and finding Lucrece attired in mourning habite, demanded the cause of her sorrow. Shee first taking an oath of them for her reuenge, reuealed the Actor, and whole maner of his dealing, and withall sodainely stabbed her selfe. Which done, with one consent they all vowed to roote out the whole hated family of the Tarquins: and bearing the dead body to Rome, Brutus acquainted the people with the doer and manner of the vile deede: with a bitter inuectiue against the tyranny of the King, wherewith the people were so moued, that with one consent and a generall acclamation, the Tarquins were all exiled, and the state gouernment changed from Kings to Consuls.

THE RAPE OF
LVCRECE.

FRom the besieged Ardea all in post,
Borne by the trustlesse wings of false desire,
　　Lust-breathed TARQVIN, leaues the Roman host,
And to Colatium beares the lightlesse fire,
VVhich in pale embers hid, lurkes to aspire,
　　And girdle with embracing flames, the wast
　　Of COLATINES fair loue, LVCRECE the chast.

Hap'ly that name of chast, vnhap'ly set
This batelesse edge on his keene appetite:
VVhen COLATINE vnwisely did not let,
To praise the cleare vnmatched red and white,
VVhich triumpht in that skie of his delight:
　　VVhere mortal stars as bright as heaues Beauties,
　　VVith pure aspects did him peculiar dueties.

B

THE RAPE OF LVCRECE,

For he the night before in Tarquins Tent,
Vnlockt the treasure of his happie ftate :
VVhat prifeleffe wealth the heauens had him lent,
In the poffeffion of his beauteous mate.
Reckning his fortune at fuch high proud rate,
   That Kings might be efpowfed to more fame,
   But King nor Peere to fuch a peereleffe dame.

O happineffe enioy'd but of a few,
And if poffeft as foone decayed and done :
As is the morning filuer melting dew,
Againft the golden fplendour of the Sunne.
An expir'd date canceld ere well begunne.
   Honour and Beautie in the owners armes,
   Are weakelie fortreft from a world of harmes.

Beautie it felfe doth of it felfe perfwade,
The eies of men without an Orator,
VVhat needeth then Appologie be made
To fet forth that which is fo finguler ?
Or why is Colatine the publifher
   Of that rich iewell he fhould keepe vnknown,
   From theeuifh eares becaufe it is his owne ?
                          Perchance

THE RAPE OF LVCRECE.

Perchance his boſt of Lucrece Sou'raigñtie,
Suggeſted this proud iſſue of a King:
For by our eares our hearts oft taynted be:
Perchance that enuie of ſo rich a thing
Brauing compare, diſdainefully did ſting   (vant,
  His high picht thoughts that meaner men ſhould
  That golden hap which their ſuperiors want.

But ſome vntimelie thought did inſtigate,
His all too timeleſſe ſpeede if none of thoſe,
His honor, his affaires, his friends, his ſtate,
Negleſted all, with ſwift intent he goes,
To quench the coale which in his liuer glowes.
  O raſh falſe heate, wrapt in repentant cold,
  Thy haſtie ſpring ſtill blaſts and nere growes old.

VVhen at Colatium this falſe Lord ariued,
VVell was he welcom'd by the Romaine dame,
VVithin whoſe face Beautie and Vertue ſtriued,
VVhich of them both ſhould vnderprop her fame.
VVhē Vertue brag'd, Beautie wold bluſh for ſhame,
  VVhen Beautie boſted bluſhes, in deſpight
  Vertue would ſtaine that ore with ſiluer white.

B 2

THE RAPE OF LVCRECE.

But Beautie in that white entituled,
From Venus doues doth challenge that faire field,
Then Vertue claimes from Beautie, Beauties red,
VVhich Vertue gaue the golden age, to guild
Their filuer cheekes, and cald it then their fhield,
　　Teaching them thus to vfe it in the fight,
　　VVhē fhame affaild, the red fhould fēce the white.

This Herauldry in LVCRECE face was feene,
Argued by Beauties red and Vertues white,
Of eithers colour was the other Queene:
Prouing from worlds minoriry their right,
Yet their ambition makes them ftill to fight:
　　The foueraignty of either being fo great,
　　That oft they interchange ech others feat.

This filent warre of Lillies and of Rofes,
VVhich TARQVIN vew'd in her faire faces field,
In their pure rankes his traytor eye enclofes,
VVhere leaft betweene them both it fhould be kild.
The coward captiue vanquifhed, doth yeeld
　　To thofe two Armies that would let him goe,
　　Rather then triumph in fo falfe a foe.
　　　　　　　　　　　　　　　　Now

66

THE RAPE OF LVCRECE.

Now thinkes he that her husbands shallow tongue,
The niggard prodigall that praisde her so :
In that high taske hath done her Beauty wrong.
VVhich farre exceedes his barren skill to show.
Therefore that praise which COLATINE doth owe,
   Inchaunted TARQVIN aunswers with surmise,
   In silent wonder of still gazing eyes.

This earthly sainct adored by this deuill,
Little suspecteth the false worshipper :
" For vntaind thoughts do seldom dream on euill.
" Birds neuer lim'd, no secret bushes feare :
So guiltlesse shee securely giues good cheare,
   And reuerend welcome to her princely guest,
   VVhose inward ill no outward harme exprest.

For that he colourd with his high estate,
Hiding base sin in pleats of Maiestie :
That nothing in him seemd inordinate,
Saue sometime too much wonder of his eye,
VVhich hauing all, all could not satisfie;
   But poorly rich so wanteth in his store,
   That cloy'd with much, he pineth still for more.

B 3

67

THE RAPE OF LVCRECE.

But she that neuer cop't with straunger eies,
Could picke no meaning from their parling lookes,
Nor read the subtie shining secrecies,
VVrit in the glassie margents of such bookes,
Shee toucht no vnknown baits, nor feard no hooks,
   Nor could shee moralize his wanton sight,
   More then his eies were opend to the light.

He stories to her eares her husbands fame,
VVonne in the fields of fruitfull Italie:
And decks with praises Colatines high name,
Made glorious by his manlie chiualrie,
VVith bruised armes and wreathes of victorie,
   Her ioie with heaued-vp hand she doth expresse,
   And wordlesse so greetes heauen for his successe.

Far from the purpose of his comming thither,
He makes excuses for his being there,
No clowdie show of stormie blustring wether,
Doth yet in his faire welkin once appeare,
Till sable Night mother of dread and feare,
   Vppon the world dim darknesse doth displaie,
   And in her vaultie prison, stowes the daie.

                            For

THE RAPE OF LVCRECE.

For then is Tarquine brought vnto his bed,
Intending wearinesse with heauie sprite:
For after supper long he questioned,
VVith modest Lucrece, and wore out the night,
Now leaden slumber with liues strength doth fight,
  And euerie one to rest himselfe betakes,
  Saue theeues, and cares, and troubled minds that
                      (wakes.

As one of which doth Tarquin lie reuoluing
The sundrie dangers of his wils obtaining:
Yet euer to obtaine his will resoluing.   (ning
Though weake-built hopes perswade him to abstai-
Dispaire to gaine doth traffique oft for gaining,
  And when great treasure is the meede proposed,
  Though death be adiūct, ther's no death supposed.

Those that much couet are with gaine so fond,
That what they haue not, that which they possesse
They scatter and vnloose it from their bond,
And so by hoping more they haue but lesse,
Or gaining more, the profite of excesse
  Is but to surfet, and such griefes sustaine,
  That they proue bāckrout in this poore rich gain.

THE RAPE OF LVCRECE.

The ayme of all is but to nourſe the life,
VVith honor, wealth, and eaſe in wainyng age:
And in this ayme there is ſuch thwarting ſtrife,
That one for all, or all for one we gage:
As life for honour, in fell battailes rage,
    Honor for wealth, and oft that wealth doth coſt
    The death of all, and altogether loſt.

So that in ventring ill, we leaue to be
The things we are, for that which we expeɛt:
And this ambitious foule infirmitie,
In hauing much torments vs with defeɛt
Of that we haue: ſo then we doe negleɛt
    The thing we haue, and all for want of wit,
    Make ſomething nothing, by augmenting it.

Such hazard now muſt doting TARQVIN make,
Pawning his honor to obtaine his luſt,
And for himſelfe, himſelfe he muſt forſake.
Then where is truth if there be no ſelfe-truſt?
VVhen ſhall he thinke to find a ſtranger iuſt,
    VVhen he himſelfe, himſelfe confounds, betraies,
    To ſclandrous tongues & wretched hateful daies?
                           Now

THE RAPE OF LVCRECE.

Now ſtole vppon the time the dead of night,
VVhen heauie ſleeep had cloſd vp mortall eyes,
No comfortable ſtarre did lend his light,
No noiſe but Owles, & wolues death-boding cries:
Now ſerues the ſeaſon that they may ſurpriſe
    The ſillie Lambes, pure thoughts are dead & ſtill,
    VVhile Luſt and Murder wakes to ſtaine and kill.

And now this luſtfull Lord leapt from his bed,
Throwing his mantle rudely ore his arme,
Is madly toſt betweene deſire and dred;
Th'one ſweetely flatters, th'other feareth harme,
But honeſt feare, bewicht with luſtes foule charme,
    Doth too too oft betake him to retire,
    Beaten away by braineſicke rude deſire.

His Faulchon on a flint he ſoftly ſmiteth,
That from the could ſtone ſparkes of fire doe flie,
VVhereat a waxen torch forthwith he lighteth,
VVhich muſt be lodeſtarre to his luſtfull eye.
And to the flame thus ſpeakes aduiſedlie;
    As from this cold flint I enforſt this fire,
    So Lvcrece muſt I force to my deſire.

                C

THE RAPE OF LVCRECE.

Here pale with feare he doth premeditate,
The daungers of his lothsome enterprise:
And in his inward mind he doth debate,
VVhat following sorrow may on this arise.
Then looking scornfully, he doth despise
   His naked armour of still slaughtered lust,
   And iustly thus controlls his thoughts vniust.

Faire torch burne out thy light, and lend it not
To darken her whose light excelleth thine:
And die vnhallowed thoughts, before you blot
VVith your vncleannesse, that which is deuine:
Offer pure incense to so pure a shrine:
   Let faire humanitie abhor the deede,
   That spots & stains loues modest snow-white weed.

O shame to knighthood, and to shining Armes,
O foule dishonor to my houshoulds graue:
O impious act including all foule harmes.
A martiall man to be soft fancies slaue,
True valour still a true respect should haue,
   Then my digression is so vile, so base,
   That it will liue engrauen in my face.

                         Yea

THE RAPE OF LVCRECE.

Yea though I die the scandale will suruiue,
And be an eie-sore in my golden coate :
Some lothsome dash the Herrald will contriue,
To cipher me how fondlie I did dote :
That my posteritie sham'd with the note
   Shall curse my bones, and hold it for no sinne,
   To wish that I their father had not beene.

VVhat win I if I gaine the thing I seeke ?
A dreame, a breath, a froth of fleeting ioy,
VVho buies a minutes mirth to waile a weeke ?
Or sels eternitie to get a toy?
For one sweete grape who will the vine destroy ?
   Or what fond begger, but to touch the crowne,
   VVould with the scepter straight be stroke down?

If COLATINVS dreame of my intent,
VVill he not wake, and in a desp'rate rage
Post hither, this vile purpose to preuent ?
This siege that hath ingirt his marriage,
This blur to youth, this sorrow to the sage,
   This dying vertue, this suruiuing shame,
   VVhose crime will beare an euer-during blame.
      C 2

THE RAPE OF LVCRECE.

O what excuſe can my inuention make
VVhen thou ſhalt charge me with ſo blacke a deed?
VVil not my tongue be mute,my fraile ioints ſhake?
Mine eies forgo their light, my falſe hart bleede?
The guilt beeing great,the feare doth ſtill exceede;
   And extreme feare can neither fight nor flie,
   But cowardlike with trembling terror die.

Had COLATINVS kild my ſonne or ſire,
Or laine in ambuſh to betray my life,
Or were he not my deare friend, this deſire
Might haue excuſe to worke vppon his wife:
As in reuenge or quittall of ſuch ſtrife.
   But as he is my kinſman, my deare friend,
   The ſhame and fault finds no excuſe nor end.

Shamefull it is : I,if the fact be knowne,
Hatefull it is : there is no hate in louing,
Ile beg her loue: but ſhe is not her owne:
The worſt is but deniall and reproouing.
My will is ſtrong paſt reaſons weake remoouing :
   VVho feares a ſentence or an old mans ſaw,
   Shall by a painted cloth be kept in awe.
                         Thus

THE RAPE OF LVCRECE.

Thus gracelesse holds he disputation,
Tweene frozen conscience and hot burning will,
And with good thoughts makes dispensation,
Vrging the worser sence for vantage still.
VVhich in a moment doth confound and kill
   All pure effects, and doth so farre proceede,
   That what is vile, shewes like a vertuous deede.

Quoth he, shee tooke me kindlie by the hand,
And gaz'd for tidings in my eager eyes,
Fearing some hard newes from the warlike band,
VVhere her beloued COLATINVS lies.
O how her feare did make her colour rise!
   First red as Roses that on Lawne we laie,
   Then white as Lawne the Roses tooke awaie.

And how her hand in my hand being lockt,
Forst it to tremble with her loyall feare:
VVhich strooke her sad, and then it faster rockt,
Vntill her husbands welfare shee did heare.
VVhereat shee smiled with so sweete a cheare,
   That had NARCISSVS seene her as shee stood,
   Selfe-loue had neuer drown'd him in the flood.

C 3

THE RAPE OF LVCRECE.

VVhy hunt I then for colour or excuses?
All Orators are dumbe when Beautie pleadeth,
Poore wretches haue remorse in poore abuses,
Loue thriues not in the hart that shadows dreadeth,
Affection is my Captaine and he leadeth.
  And when his gaudie banner is displaide,
  The coward fights, and will not be dismaide.

Then childish feare auaunt, debating die,
Respect and reason waite on wrinckled age:
My heart shall neuer countermand mine eie;
Sad pause, and deepe regard beseemes the sage,
My part is youth and beates these from the stage.
  Desire my Pilot is, Beautie my prise,
  Then who feares sinking where such treasure lies?

As corne ore-growne by weedes: so heedfull feare
Is almost choakt by vnresisted lust:
Away he steales with open listning eare,
Full of foule hope, and full of fond mistrust:
Both which as seruitors to the vniust,
  So crosse him with their opposit perswasion,
  That now he vowes a league, and now inuasion.

                    VVith-

THE RAPE OF LVCRECE.

VVithin his thought her heauenly image sits,
And in the selfe same seat sits COLATINE,
That eye which lookes on her confounds his wits,
That eye which him beholdes, as more deuine,
Vnto a view so false will not incline;
    But with a pure appeale seekes to the heart,
    VVhich once corrupted takes the worser part.

And therein heartens vp his seruile powers,
VVho flattred by their leaders iocound show,
Stuffe vp his lust : as minutes fill vp howres.
And as their Captaine: so their pride doth grow,
Paying more slauish tribute then they owe.
    By reprobate desire thus madly led,
    The Romane Lord marcheth to LVCRECE bed.

The lockes betweene her chamber and his will,
Ech one by him inforst retires his ward :
But as they open they all rate his ill,
VVhich driues the creeping theefe to some regard,
The threshold grates the doore to haue him heard,
    Night-wandring weezels shreek to see him there,
    They fright him, yet he still pursues his feare.

THE RAPE OF LVCRECE.

As each vnwilling portall yeelds him way,
Through little vents and cranies of the place,
The wind warres with his torch, to make him ſtaie,
And blowes the ſmoake of it into his face,
Extinguiſhing his conduct in this caſe.
　But his hot heart, which fond deſire doth ſcorch,
　Puffes forth another wind that fires the torch.

And being lighted, by the light he ſpies
LVCRECIAS gloue, wherein her needle ſticks,
He takes it from the ruſhes where it lies,
And griping it, the needle his finger pricks.
As who ſhould ſay, this gloue to wanton trickes
　Is not inur'd; returne againe in haſt,
　Thou ſeeſt our miſtreſſe ornaments are chaſt.

But all theſe poore forbiddings could not ſtay him,
He in the worſt ſence conſters their deniall:
The dores, the wind, the gloue that did delay him,
He takes for accidentall things of triall.
Or as thoſe bars which ſtop the hourely diall,
　VVho with a lingring ſtaie his courſe doth let,
　Till euerie minute payes the howre his debt.

　　　　　　　　　　　　　　　　　　So

78

THE RAPE OF LVCRECE.

So fo, quoth he, thefe lets attend the time,
Like little frofts that fometime threat the fpring,
To ad a more reioyfing to the prime,
And giue the fneaped birds more caufe to fing.
Pain payes the income of ech precious thing, (fands
 Huge rocks, high winds, ftrong pirats, fhelues and
 The marchant feares, ere rich at home he lands.

Now is he come vnto the chamber dore,
That fhuts him from the Heauen of his thought,
VVhich with a yeelding latch, and with no more,
Hath bard him from the bleffed thing he fought.
So from himfelfe impiety hath wrought,
 That for his pray to pray he doth begin,
 As if the Heauens fhould countenance his fin.

But in the midft of his vnfruitfull prayer,
Hauing folicited th'eternall power,
That his foule thoughts might côpaffe his fair faire,
And they would ftand aufpicious to the howre.
Euen there he ftarts, quoth he, I muft deflowre;
 The powers to whom I pray abhor this fact,
 How can they then affift me in the act?

   D

THE RAPE OF LVCRECE.

Then Loue and Fortune be my Gods, my guide,
My will is backt with refolution:
Thoughts are but dreames till their effects be tried,
The blackeft finne is clear'd with abfolution.
Againft loues fire, feares froft hath diffolution.
    The eye of Heauen is out, and miftie night
    Couers the fhame that followes fweet delight.

This faid, his guiltie hand pluckt vp the latch,
And with his knee the dore he opens wide,
The doue fleeps faft that this night Owle will catch.
Thus treafon workes ere traitors be efpied.
    VVho fees the lurking ferpent fteppes afide;
    But fhee found fleeping fearing no fuch thing,
    Lies at the mercie of his mortall fting.

Into the chamber wickedlie he ftalkes,
And gazeth on her yet vnftained bed:
The curtaines being clofe, about he walkes,
Rowling his greedie eye-bals in his head.
By their high treafon is his heart mif-led,
    VVhich giues the watch-word to his hand ful foon,
    To draw the clowd that hides the filuer Moon.

                      Looke

THE RAPE OF LVCRECE.

Looke as the faire and fierie pointed Sunne,
Rushing from forth a cloud, bereaues our sight:
Euen so the Curtaine drawne, his eyes begun
To winke, being blinded with a greater light.
VVhether it is that shee reflects so bright,
  That dazleth them, or else some shame supposed,
  But blind they are, and keep themselues inclosed.

O had they in that darkesome prison died,
Then had they seene the period of their ill:
Then COLATINE againe by LVCRECE side,
In his cleare bed might haue reposed still.
But they must ope this blessed league to kill,
  And holie-thoughted LVCRECE to their sight,
  Must sell her ioy, her life, her worlds delight.

Her lillie hand, her rosie cheeke lies vnder,
Coosning the pillow of a lawfull kisse:
VVho therefore angrie seemes to part in sunder,
Swelling on either side to want his blisse.
Betweene whose hils her head intombed is;
  VVhere like a vertuous Monument shee lies,
  To be admir'd of lewd vnhallowed eyes.

D 2

THE RAPE OF LVCRECE.

VVithout the bed her other faire hand was,
On the greene couerlet whose perfect white
Showed like an Aprill dazie on the grasse,
VVith pearlie swet resembling dew of night.
Her eyes like Marigolds had sheath'd their light,
   And canopied in darkenesse sweetly lay,
   Till they might open to adorne the day.

Her haire like goldē threeds playd with her breath,
O modest wantons, wanton modestie!
Showing lifes triumph in the map of death,
And deaths dim looke in lifes mortalitie.
Ech in her sleepe themselues so beautifie,
   As if betweene them twaine there were no strife,
   But that life liu'd in death, and death in life.

Her breasts like Iuory globes circled with blew,
A paire of maiden worlds vnconquered,
Saue of their Lord, no bearing yoke they knew,
And him by oath they truely honored.
These worlds in TARQVIN new ambition bred,
   VVho like a fowle vsurper went about,
   From this faire throne to heaue the owner out.

                          VVhat

THE RAPE OF LVCRECE.

VVhat could he see but mightily he noted?
VVhat did he note, but ftrongly he defired?
VVhat he beheld, on that he firmely doted,
And in his will his wilfull eye he tyred.
VVith more then admiration he admired
   Her azure vaines, her alablafter skinne,
   Her corall lips, her fnow-white dimpled chin.

As the grim Lion fawneth ore his pray,
Sharpe hunger by the conqueft fatisfied:
So ore this fleeping foule doth TARQVIN ftay,
His rage of luft by gazing qualified;
Slakt, not fuppreft, for ftanding by her fide,
   His eye which late this mutiny reftraines,
   Vnto a greater vprore tempts his vaines.

And they like ftragling flaues for pillage fighting,
Obdurate vaffals fell exploits effecting,
In bloudy death and rauifhment delighting;
Nor childrens tears nor mothers grones refpecting,
Swell in their pride, the onfet ftill expecting:
   Anon his beating heart allarum ftriking,
   Giues the hot charge, & bids thē do their liking.

D 3

THE RAPE OF LVCRECE.

His drumming heart cheares vp his burning eye,
His eye commends the leading to his hand;
His hand as proud of such a dignitie,
Smoaking with pride, marcht on, to make his stand
On her bare brest, the heart of all her land;
 VVhose ranks of blew vains as his hand did scale,
 Left their round turrets destitute and pale.

They mustring to the quiet Cabinet,
VVhere their deare gouernesse and ladie lies,
Do tell her shee is dreadfullie beset,
And fright her with confusion of their cries.
Shee much amaz'd breakes ope her lockt vp eyes,
 VVho peeping foorth this tumult to behold,
 Are by his flaming torch dim'd and controld.

Imagine her as one in dead of night,
From forth dull sleepe by dreadfull fancie waking,
That thinkes shee hath beheld some gastlie sprite,
VVhose grim aspect sets euerie ioint a shaking,
VVhat terror tis : but shee in worser taking,
 From sleepe disturbed, heedfullie doth view
 The sight which makes supposed terror trew.

            VVrapt

THE RAPE OF LVCRECE.

VVrapt and confounded in a thousand feares,
Like to a new-kild bird shee trembling lies:
Shee dares not looke, yet winking there appeares
Quicke-shifting Antiques vglie in her eyes.
" Such shadowes are the weake-brains forgeries,
    VVho angrie that the eyes flie from their lights,
    In darknes daunts thē with more dreadfull sights.

His hand that yet remaines vppon her brest,
(Rude Ram to batter such an Iuorie wall:)
May feele her heart (poore Cittizen) distrest,
VVounding it selfe to death, rise vp and fall;
Beating her bulke, that his hand shakes withall.
    This moues in him more rage and lesser pittie,
    To make the breach and enter this sweet Citty.

First like a Trompet doth his tongue begin,
To sound a parlie to his heartlesse foe,
VVho ore the white sheet peers her whiter chin,
The reason of this rash allarme to know,
VVhich he by dum demeanor seekes to show.
    But shee with vehement prayers vrgeth still,
    Vnder what colour he commits this ill.

THE RAPE OF LVCRECE.

Thus he replies, the colour in thy face,
That euen for anger makes the Lilly pale,
And the red rose blush at her owne disgrace,
Shall plead for me and tell my louing tale.
Vnder that colour am I come to scale
   Thy neuer conquered Fort, the fault is thine,
   For those thine eyes betray thee vnto mine.

Thus I forestall thee, if thou meane to chide,
Thy beauty hath ensnar'd thee to this night,
VVhere thou with patience must my will abide,
My will that markes thee for my earths delight,
VVhich I to conquer sought with all my might.
   But as reproofe and reason beat it dead,
   By thy bright beautie was it newlie bred.

I see what crosses my attempt will bring,
I know what thornes the growing rose defends,
I thinke the honie garded with a sting,
All this before-hand counsell comprehends.
But VVill is deafe, and hears no heedfull friends,
   Onely he hath an eye to gaze on Beautie,
   And dotes on what he looks, gainst law or duety.

I

THE RAPE OF LVCRECE.

I haue debated euen in my soule,
VVhat wrong, what shame, what sorrow I shal breed,
But nothing can affections course controull,
Or stop the headlong furie of his speed.
I know repentant teares insewe the deed,
  Reproch, disdaine, and deadly enmity,
  Yet striue I to embrace mine infamy.

This said, hee shakes aloft his Romaine blade,
VVhich like a Faulcon towring in the skies,
Cowcheth the fowle below with his wings sha de,
VVhose crooked beake threats, if he mount he dies.
So vnder his insulting Fauchion lies
  Harmelesse LVCRETIA marking what he tels,
  VVith trembling feare: as fowl hear Faulcōs bels.

LVCRECE, quoth he, this night I must enioy thee,
If thou deny, then force must worke my way :
For in thy bed I purpose to destroie thee.
That done, some worthlesse slaue of thine ile slay.
To kill thine Honour with thy liues decaie.
  And in thy dead armes do I meane to place him,
  Swearing I slue him seeing thee imbrace him.

E

THE RAPE OF LVCRECE.

So thy furuiuing husband fhall remaine
The fcornefull marke of euerie open eye,
Thy kinfmen hang their heads at this difdaine,
Thy iffue blur'd with namelefe baftardie;
And thou the author of their obloquie,
   Shalt haue thy trefpaffe cited vp in rimes,
   And fung by children in fucceeding times.

But if thou yeeld, I reft thy fecret friend,
The fault vnknowne, is as a thought vnacted,
" A little harme done to a great good end,
For lawfull pollicie remaines enacted.
" The poyfonous fimple fometime is compacted
   In a pure compound; being fo applied,
   His venome in effect is purified.

Then for thy husband and thy childrens fake,
Tender my fuite, bequeath not to their lot
The fhame that from them no deuife can take,
The blemifh that will neuer be forgot:
VVorfe then a flauifh wipe, or birth howrs blot,
   For markes difcried in mens natiuitie,
   Are natures faultes, not their owne infamie.

Here

THE RAPE OF LVCRECE.

Here with a Cockeatrice dead killing eye,
He rowseth vp himselfe, and makes a pause,
VVhile shee the picture of pure pietie,
Like a white Hinde vnder the grypes sharpe clawes,
Pleades in a wildernesse where are no lawes,
 To the rough beast, that knowes no gentle right,
 Nor ought obayes but his fowle appetite.

But when a black-fac'd clowd the world doth thret,
In his dim mist th'aspiring mountaines hiding:
From earths dark-womb, some gentle gust doth get,
VVhich blow these pitchie vapours frō their biding:
Hindring their present fall by this deuiding.
 So his vnhallowed hast her words delayes,
 And moodie PLVTO winks while Orpheus playes.

Yet fowle night-waking Cat he doth but dallie,
VVhile in his hold-fast foot the weak mouse pāteth,
Her sad behauiour feedes his vulture follie,
A swallowing gulfe that euen in plentie wanteth.
His eare her prayers admits, but his heart granteth
 No penetrable entrance to her playning,
 "Tears harden lust though marble were with ray-
     E 2   (ning.

89

THE RAPE OF LVCRECE.

Her pittie-pleading eyes are sadlie fixed
In the remorselesse wrinckles of his face.
Her modest eloquence with sighes is mixed,
VVhich to her Oratorie addes more grace.
Shee puts the period often from his place,
   And midst the sentence so her accent breakes,
   That twise she doth begin ere once she speakes.

She coniures him by high Almightie Ioue,
By knighthood, gentrie, and sweete friendships oth,
By her vntimely teares, her husbands loue,
By holie humaine law, and common troth,
By Heauen and Earth, and all the power of both :
   That to his borrowed bed he make retire,
   And stoope to Honor, not to fowle desire.

Quoth shee, reward not Hospitalitie,
VVith such black payment, as thou hast pretended,
Mudde not the fountaine that gaue drinke to thee,
Mar not the thing that cannot be amended.
End thy ill ayme, before thy shoote be ended.
   He is no wood-man that doth bend his bow,
   To strike a poore vnseasonable Doe.

                                  My

THE RAPE OF LVCRECE.

My husband is thy friend, for his fake fpare me,
Thy felfe art mightie, for thine own fake leaue me:
My felfe a weakling, do not then infnare me.
Thou look'ft not like deceipt, do not deceiue me.
My fighes like whirlewindes labor hence to heaue
  If euer man were mou'd with womãs mones, (thee.
  Be moued with my teares, my fighes, my grones.

All which together like a troubled Ocean,
Beat at thy rockie, and wracke-threatning heart,
To foften it with their continuall motion:
For ftones diffolu'd to water do conuert.
O if no harder then a ftone thou art,
  Melt at my teares and be compaffionate,
  Soft pittie enters at an iron gate.

In TARQVINS likeneffe I did entertaine thee,
Haft thou put on his fhape, to do him fhame?
To all the Hoft of Heauen I complaine me.
Thou wrongft his honor, woũdft his princely name:
Thou art not what thou feem'ft, and if the fame,
  Thou feem'ft not what thou art, a God, a King;
  For kings like Gods fhould gouerne euery thing.

E 3

THE RAPE OF LVCRECE.

How will thy fhame be feeded in thine age
VVhen thus thy vices bud before thy ſpring?
If in thy hope thou darſt do ſuch outrage,
VVhat dar'ſt thou not when once thou art a King?
O be remembred, no outragious thing
  From vaſſall actors can be wipt away,
  Then Kings miſdeedes cannot be hid in clay.

This deede will make thee only lou'd for feare,
But happie Monarchs ſtill are feard for loue:
VVith fowle offendors thou perforce muſt beare,
VVhen they in thee the like offences proue;
If but for feare of this, thy will remoue.
  For Princes are the glaſſe, the ſchoole, the booke,
  VVhere ſubiects eies do learn, do read, do looke.

And wilt thou be the ſchoole where luſt ſhall learne?
Muſt he in thee read lectures of ſuch ſhame?
VVilt thou be glaſſe wherein it ſhall diſcerne
Authoritie for ſinne, warrant for blame?
To priuiledge diſhonor in thy name.
  Thou backſt reproch againſt long-liuing lawd,
  And mak'ſt faire reputation but a bawd.

                        Haſt

THE RAPE OF LVCRECE.

Haft thou commaund ? by him that gaue it thee
From a pure heart commaund thy rebell will :
Draw not thy fword to gard iniquitie,
For it was lent thee all that broode to kill.
Thy Princelie office how canft thou fulfill ?
  VVhen patternd by thy fault fowle fin may fay,
  He learnd to fin, and thou didft teach the way.

Thinke but how vile a fpectacle it were,
To view thy prefent trefpaffe in another :
Mens faults do feldome to themfelues appeare,
Their own tranfgreffions partiallie they fmother,
This guilt would feem death-worthie in thy brother.
  O how are they wrapt in with infamies,
  That frŏ their own mifdeeds askaunce their eyes?

To thee, to thee, my heau'd vp hands appeale,
Not to feducing luft thy rafh relier:
I fue for exil'd maiefties repeale,
Let him returne, and flattring thoughts retire.
His true refpect will prifon falfe defire,
  And wipe the dim mift from thy doting eien,
  That thou fhalt fee thy ftate, and pittie mine.

THE RAPE OF LV.CRECE.

Haue done, quoth he, my vncontrolled tide
Turnes not, but fwels the higher by this let.
Small lightes are foone blown out, huge fires abide,
And with the winde in greater furie fi et:
The petty ftreames that paie a dailie det
    To their falt foueraigne with their frefh fals haft,
    Adde to his flowe, but alter not his taft.

Thou art, quoth fhee, a fea, a foueraigne King,
And loe there fals into thy boundlefle flood,
Blacke luft, difhonor, fhame, mif-gouerning,
VVho feeke to ftaine the Ocean of thy blood.
If all thefe pettie ils fhall change thy good,
    Thy fea within a puddels wombe is herféd,
    And not the puddle in thy fea difperfed.

So fhall thefe flaues be King, and thou their flaue,
Thou noblie bafe, they bafelie dignified:
Thou their faire life, and they thy fowler graue:
Thou lothed in their fhame, they in thy pride,
The lefter thing fhould not the greater hide.
    The Cedar ftoopes not to the bafe fhrubs foote,
    But low-fhrubs wither at the Cedars roote.

                      So

THE RAPE OF LVCRECE.

So let thy thoughts low vaſſals to thy ſtate,
No more quoth he, by Heauen I will not heare thee.
Yeeld to my loue, if not inforced hate,
In ſteed of loues coy tutch ſhall rudelie teare thee.
That done, deſpitefullie I meane to beare thee
   Vnto the baſe bed of ſome raſcall groome,
   To be thy partner in this ſhamefull doome.

This ſaid, he ſets his foote vppon the light,
For light and luſt are deadlie enemies,
Shame folded vp in blind concealing night,
VVhen moſt vnſeene, then moſt doth tyrannize.
The wolfe hath ceazd his pray, the poor lamb cries,
   Till with her own white fleece her voice controld,
   Intombes her outcrie in her lips ſweet fold.

For with the nightlie linnen that ſhee weares,
He pens her piteous clamors in her head,
Cooling his hot face in the chaſteſt teares,
That euer modeſt eyes with ſorrow ſhed.
O that prone luſt ſhould ſtaine ſo pure a bed,
   The ſpots whereof could weeping purifie,
   Her tears ſhould drop on them perpetuallie.

F

THE RAPE OF LVCRECE.

But shee hath lost a dearer thing then life,
And he hath wonne what he would loose againe,
This forced league doth force a further strife,
This momentarie ioy breeds months of paine,
This hot desire conuerts to colde disdaine;
   Pure chastitie is rifled of her store,
   And lust the theefe farre poorer then before.

Looke as the full-fed Hound, or gorged Hawke,
Vnapt for tender smell, or speedie flight,
Make slow pursuite, or altogether bauk,
The praie wherein by nature they delight:
So surfet-taking TARQVIN fares this night:
   His tast delicious, in digestion sowring,
   Deuoures his will that liu'd by fowle deuouring.

O deeper sinne then bottomlesse conceit
Can comprehend in still imagination!
Drunken Desire must vomite his receipt
Ere he can see his owne abhomination.
VVhile Lust is in his pride no exclamation
   Can curbe his heat, or reine his rash desire,
   Till like a Iade, self-will himselfe doth tire.

                          And

THE RAPE OF LVCRECE.

And then with lanke, and leane difcolour'd cheeke,
VVith heauie eye, knit-brow, and ftrengthleffe pace,
Feeble defire all recreant, poore and meeke,
Like to a banckrout begger wailes his cace:
The flefh being proud, Defire doth fight with grace;
   For there it reuels, and when that decaies,
   The guiltie rebell for remiffion praies.

So fares it with this fault-full Lord of Rome,
VVho this accomplifhment fo hotly chafed,
For now againft himfelfe he founds this doome,
That through the length of times he ftads difgraced:
Befides his foules faire temple is defaced,
   To whofe weake ruines mufter troopes of cares,
   To aske the fpotted Princeffe how fhe fares.

Shee fayes her fubiects with fowle infurrection,
Haue batterd downe her confecrated wall,
And by their mortall fault brought in fubiection
Her immortalitie, and made her thrall,
To liuing death and payne perpetuall.
   VVhich in her prefcience fhee controlled ftill,
   But her forefight could not foreftall their will.

F 2

THE RAPE OF LVCRECE.

Eu'n in this thought through the dark-night he ſtea-
A captiue victor that hath loſt in gaine,   (leth,
Bearing away the wound that nothing healeth,
The ſcarre that will diſpight of Cure remaine,
Leauing his ſpoile perplext in greater paine.
   Shee beares the lode of luſt he left behinde,
   And he the burthen of a guiltie minde.

Hee like a theeuiſh dog creeps ſadly thence,
Shee like a wearied Lambe lies panting there,
He ſcowles and hates himſelfe for his offence,
Shee deſperat with her nailes her fleſh doth teare.
He faintly flies ſweating with guiltie feare;
   Shee ſtaies exclayming on the direfull night,
   He runnes and chides his vaniſht loth'd delight.

He thence departs a heauy conuertite,
Shee there remaines a hopeleſſe caſt-away,
He in his ſpeed lookes for the morning light:
Shee prayes ſhee neuer may behold the day.
For daie, quoth ſhee, nights ſcapes doth open lay,
   And my true eyes haue neuer practiz'd how
   To cloake offences with a cunning brow.

                 They

THE RAPE OF LVCRECE.

They thinke not but that euerie eye can fee,
The fame difgrace which they themfelues behold :
And therefore would they ftill in darkeneffe be,
To haue their vnfeene finne remaine vntold.
For they their guilt with weeping will vnfold,
   And graue like water that doth eate in fteele,
   Vppon my cheeks, what helpeleffe fhame I feele.

Here fhee exclaimes againft repofe and reft,
And bids her eyes hereafter ftill be blinde,
Shee wakes her heart by beating on her breft,
And bids it leape from thence, where it maie finde
Some purer cheft, to clofe fo pure a minde.
   Franticke with griefe thus breaths fhee forth her
   Againft the vnfeene fecrecie of night.   (fpite,

O comfort-killing night, image of Hell,
Dim regifter, and notarie of fhame;
Blacke ftage for tragedies, and murthers fell,
Vaft fin-concealing Chaos, nourfe of blame.
Blinde muffled bawd, darke harber for defame,
   Grim caue of death, whifpring confpirator,
   VVith clofe-tong'd treafon & the rauifher.

F 3

THE RAPE OF LVCRECE.

O hatefull, vaporous, and foggy night,
Since thou art guilty of my cureleſſe crime:
Muſter thy miſts to meete the Eaſterne light,
Make war againſt proportion'd courſe of time.
Or if thou wilt permit the Sunne to clime
   His wonted height, yet ere he go to bed,
   Knit poyſonous clouds about his golden head.

VVith rotten damps rauiſh the morning aire,
Let their exhald vnholdſome breaths make ſicke
The life of puritie, the ſupreme faire,
Ere he arriue his wearie noone-tide pricke,
And let thy muſtie vapours march ſo thicke,
   That in their ſmoakie rankes, his ſmothred light
   May ſet at noone, and make perpetuall night.

VVere TARQVIN night, as he is but nights child,
The ſiluer ſhining Queene he would diſtaine;
Her twinckling handmaids to (by him defil'd)
Through nights black boſom ſhuld not peep again.
So ſhould I haue copartners in my paine,
   And fellowſhip in woe doth woe aſſwage,
   As Palmers chat makes ſhort their pilgrimage.
                       VVhere

THE RAPE OF LVCRECE

VVhere now I haue no one to blush with me,
To croffe their armes & hang their heads with mine,
To maske their browes and hide their infamie,
But I alone, alone muft fit and pine,
Seafoning the earth with fhowres of filuer brine;
 Mingling my talk with tears, my greef with grones,
 Poore wafting monuments of lafting mones.

O night thou furnace of fowle reeking fmoke!
Let not he iealous daie behold that face,
VVhich vnderneath thy blacke all-hiding cloke
Immodeftly lies martird with difgrace.
Keepe ftill poffeffion of thy gloomy place,
 That all the faults which in thy raigne are made,
 May likewife be fepulcherd in thy fhade.

Make me not obiect to the tell-tale day,
The light will fhew charaçterd in my brow,
The ftorie of fweete chaftities decay,
The impious breach of holy wedlocke vowe.
Yea the illiterate that know not how
 To cipher what is writ in learned bookes,
 VVill cote my lothfome trefpaffe in my lookes.

THE RAPE OF LVCRECE.

The nourſe to ſtill her child will tell my ſtorie,
And fright her crying babe with T A R Q V I N S name.
The Orator to decke his oratorie,
VVill couple my reproch to T A R Q V I N S ſhame.
Feaſt-finding minſtrels tuning my defame,
 VVill tie the hearers to attend ech line,
 How T A R Q V I N wronged me, I C O L A T I N E.

Let my good name, that ſenceleſſe reputation,
For C O L A T I N E S deare loue be kept vnſpotted:
If that be made a theame for diſputation,
The branches of another roote are rotted;
And vndeſeru'd reproch to him alotted,
 That is as cleare from this attaint of mine,
 As I ere this was pure to C O L A T I N E.

O vnſeene ſhame, inuiſible diſgrace,
O vnfelt ſore, creſt-wounding priuat ſcarre!
Reproch is ſtampt in C O L A T I N V S face,
And T A R Q V I N S eye maie read the mot a farre,
"How he in peace is wounded not in warre.
 "Alas how manie beare ſuch ſhamefull blowes,
 VVhich not thēſelues but he that giues thē knowes.

            If

THE RAPE OF LVCRECE.

If Colatine, thine honor laie in me,
From me by strong assault it is bereft:
My Honnie lost, and I a Drone-like Bee,
Haue no perfection of my sommer left,
But rob'd and ransak't by iniurious theft.
   In thy weake Hiue a wandring waspe hath crept,
   And suck't the Honnie which thy chast Bee kept.

Yet am I guiltie of thy Honors wracke,
Yet for thy Honor did I entertaine him,
Comming from thee I could not put him backe:
For it had beene dishonor to disdaine him,
Besides of wearinesse he did complaine him,
   And talk't of Vertue (O vnlook't for euill,)
   VVhen Vertue is prophan'd in such a Deuill.

VVhy should the worme intrude the maiden bud?
Or hatefull Kuckcowes hatch in Sparrows nests?
Or Todes infect faire founts with venome mud?
Or tyrant follie lurke in gentle brests?
Or Kings be breakers of their owne beheftes?
   "But no perfection is so absolute,
   That some impuritie doth not pollute.
        G

THE RAPE OF LVCRECE.

The aged man that coffers vp his gold,
Is plagu'd with cramps, and gouts,and painefull fits,
And scarce hath eyes his treasure to behold,
But like still pining TANTALVS he sits,
And vselesse barnes the haruest of his wits:
   Hauing no other pleasure of his gaine,
   But torment that it cannot cure his paine.

So then he hath it when he cannot vse it,
And leaues it to be maistred by his yong:
VVho in their pride do presently abuse it,
Their father was too weake, and they too strong
To hold their cursed-blessed Fortune long.
   " The sweets we wish for, turne to lothed sowrs,
   " Euen in the moment that we call them ours.

Vnruly blasts wait on the tender spring,
Vnholsome weeds take roote with precious flowrs,
The Adder hisses where the sweete birds sing,
VVhat Vertue breedes Iniquity deuours:
VVe haue no good that we can say is ours,
   But ill annexed opportunity
   Or kils his life, or else his quality.

O

THE RAPE OF LVCRECE.

O opportunity thy guilt is great,
Tis thou that execur'ft the traytors treafon:
Thou fets the wolfe where he the lambe may get,
VVho euer plots the finne thou poinft the feafon.
Tis thou that fpurn'ft at right, at law, at reafon,
   And in thy fhadie Cell where none may fpie him,
   Sits fin to ceaze the foules that wander by him.

Thou makeft the veftall violate her oath,
Thou bloweft the fire when temperance is thawd,
Thou fmotherft honeftie, thou murthreft troth,
Thou fowle abbettor, thou notorious bawd,
Thou planteft fcandall, and difplaceft lawd.
   Thou rauifher, thou traytor, thou falfe theefe,
   Thy honie turnes to gall, thy ioy to greefe.

Thy fecret pleafure turnes to open fhame,
Thy priuate feafting to a publicke faft,
Thy fmoothing titles to a ragged name,
Thy fugred tongue to bitter wormwood taft,
Thy violent vanities can neuer laft.
   How comes it then, vile opportunity
   Being fo bad, fuch numbers feeke for thee?

G 2

THE RAPE OF LVCRECE.

VVhen wilt thou be the humble suppliants friend
And bring him where his suit may be obtained?
VVhen wilt thou sort an howre great strifes to end?
Or free that soule which wretchednes hath chained?
Giue phisicke to the sicke, ease to the pained?
   The poore, lame, blind, hault, creepe, cry out for
   But they nere meet with oportunitie.   (thee,

The patient dies while the Phisitian sleepes,
The Orphane pines while the oppressor feedes.
Iustice is feasting while the widow weepes.
Aduise is sporting while infection breeds.
Thou graunt'st no time for charitable deeds.
   VVrath, enuy, treason, rape, and murthers rages,
   Thy heinous houres wait on them as their Pages.

VVhen Trueth and Vertue haue to do with thee,
A thousand crosses keepe them from thy aide:
They buie thy helpe, but sinne nere giues a fee,
He gratis comes, and thou art well apaide,
As well to heare, as graunt what he hath saide.
   My COLATINE would else haue come to me,
   VVhen TARQVIN did, but he was staied by thee.

                    Guilty

THE RAPE OF LVCRECE.

Guilty thou art of murther, and of theft,
Guilty of periurie, and subornation,
Guilty of treason, forgerie, and shift,
Guilty of incest that abhomination,
An accessarie by thine inclination.
 To all sinnes past and all that are to come,
 From the creation to the generall doome.

Misshapen time, copesmate of vgly night,
Swift subtle post, carrier of grieslie care,
Eater of youth, false slaue to false delight:
Base watch of woes, sins packhorse, vertues snare.
Thou noursest all, and murthrest all that are.
 O heare me then, iniurious shifting time,
 Be guiltie of my death since of my crime.

VVhy hath thy seruant opportunity
Betraide the howres thou gau'st me to repose?
Canceld my fortunes, and inchained me
To endlesse date of neuer-ending woes?
Times office is to fine the hate of foes,
 To eate vp errours by opinion bred,
 Not spend the dowrie of a lawfull bed.

G 3

THE RAPE OF LVCRECE.

Times glorie is to calme contending Kings,
To vnmaske falshood, and bring truth to light,
To stampe the seale of time in aged things,
To wake the morne, and Centinell the night,
To wrong the wronger till he render right,
   To ruinate proud buildings with thy howres,
   And smeare with dust their glitring golden towrs.

To fill with worme-holes stately monuments,
To feede obliuion with decay of things,
To blot old bookes, and alter their contents,
To plucke the quils from auncient rauens wings,
To drie the old oakes sappe, and cherish springs :
   To spoile Antiquities of hammerd steele,
   And turne the giddy round of Fortunes wheele.

To shew the beldame daughters of her daughter,
To make the child a man, the man a childe,
To slay the tygre that doth liue by slaughter,
To tame the Vnicorne, and Lion wild,
To mocke the subtle in themselues beguild,
   To cheare the Plowman with increasefull crops,
   And wast huge stones with little water drops.

                             VVhy

THE RAPE OF LVCRECE.

VVhy work'ſt thou miſchiefe in thy Pilgrimage,
Vnleſſe thou could'ſt returne to make amends?
One poore retyring minute in an age
VVould purchaſe thee a thouſand thouſand friends,
Lending him wit that to bad detters lends, (backe,
 O this dread night, would'ſt thou one howr come
 I could preuent this ſtorme, and ſhun thy wracke.

Thou ceaſeleſſe lackie to Eternitie,
VVith ſome miſchance croſſe TARQVIN in his flight.
Deuiſe extreames beyond extremitie,
To make him curſe this curſed crimefull night:
Let gaſtly ſhadowes his lewd eyes affright,
 And the dire thought of his committed euill,
 Shape euery buſh a hideous ſhapeleſſe deuill.

Diſturbe his howres of reſt with reſtleſſe trances,
Afflict him in his bed with bedred grones,
Let there bechaunce him pitifull miſchances,
To make him mone, but pitie not his mones:
Stone him with hardned hearts harder then ſtones,
 And let milde women to him looſe their mildneſſe,
 VVilder to him then Tygers in their wildneſſe.

THE RAPE OF LVCRECE.

Let him haue time to teare his curled haire,
Let him haue time againſt himſelfe to raue,
Let him haue time of times helpe to diſpaire,
Let him haue time to liue a lothed ſlaue,
Let him haue time a beggers orts to craue,
   And time to ſee one that by almes doth liue,
   Diſdaine to him diſdained ſcraps to giue.

Let him haue time to ſee his friends his foes,
And merrie fooles to mocke at him reſort:
Let him haue time to marke how ſlow time goes
In time of ſorrow, and how ſwift and ſhort
His time of follie, and his time of ſport.
   And euer let his vnrecalling crime
   Haue time to waile th'abuſing of his time.

O time thou tutor both to good and bad,
Teach me to curſe him that thou taught'ſt this ill :
At his owne ſhadow let the theeſe runne mad,
Himſelfe, himſelfe ſeeke euerie howre to kill,
Such wretched hãds ſuch wretched blood ſhuld ſpill.
   For who ſo baſe would ſuch an office haue,
   As ſclandrous deaths-man to ſo baſe a ſlaue.

                          The

THE RAPE OF LVCRECE.

The baſer is he comming from a King,
To ſhame his hope with deedes degenerate,
The mightier man the mightier is the thing
That makes him honord, or begets him hate:
For greateſt ſcandall waits on greateſt ſtate.
    The Moone being clouded, preſently is miſt,
    But little ſtars may hide them when they liſt.

The Crow may bath his coaleblacke wings in mire,
And vnperceau'd flie with the filth away,
But if the like the ſnow-white Swan deſire,
The ſtaine vppon his ſiluer Downe will ſtay.
Poore grooms are ſightles night, kings glorious day,
    Gnats are vnnoted whereſoere they flie,
    But Eagles gaz'd vppon with euerie eye.

Out idle wordes, ſeruants to ſhallow fooles,
Vnprofitable ſounds, weake arbitrators,
Buſie your ſelues in skill contending ſchooles,
Debate where leyſure ſerues with dull debators:
To trembling Clients be you mediators,
    For me, I force not argument a ſtraw,
    Since that my caſe is paſt the helpe of law.

H

THE RAPE OF LVCRECE.

In vaine I raile at oportunitie,
At time, at TARQVIN, and vnchearfull night,
In vaine I cauill with mine infamie,
In vaine I spurne at my confirm'd despight,
This helpelesse smoake of words doth me no right:
 The remedie indeede to do me good,
 Is to let forth my fowle defiled blood.

Poore hand why quiuerst thou at this decree?
Honor thy selfe to rid me of this shame,
For if I die, my Honor liues in thee,
But if I liue thou liu'st in my defame;
Since thou couldst not defend thy loyall Dame,
 And wast affeard to scratch her wicked Fo,
 Kill both thy selfe, and her for yeelding so.

This said, from her betombled couch shee starteth,
To finde some desp'rat Instrument of death,
But this no slaughter house no toole imparteth,
To make more vent for passage of her breath,
VVhich thronging through her lips so vanisheth,
 As smoake from ÆTNA, that in aire consumes,
 Or that which from discharged Cannon fumes.

         In

THE RAPE OF LVCRECE.

In vaine (quoth shee) I liue, and seeke in vaine
Some happie meane to end a haplesse life.
I fear'd by TARQVINS Fauchion to be slaine,
Yet for the selfe same purpose seeke a knife;
But when I fear'd I was a loyall wife,
    So am I now, ô no that cannot be,
    Of that true tipe hath TARQVIN rifled me.

O that is gone for which I sought to liue,
And therefore now I need not feare to die,
To cleare this spot by death (at least) I giue
A badge of Fame to sclanders liuerie,
A dying life, to liuing infamie:
    Poore helplesse helpe, the treasure stolne away,
    To burne the guiltlesse casket where it lay.

VVell well deare COLATINE, thou shalt not know
The stained tast of violated troth:
I will not wrong thy true affection so,
To flatter thee with an infringed oath:
This bastard graffe shall neuer come to growth,
    He shall not boast who did thy stocke pollute,
    That thou art doting father of his fruite.

H 2

THE RAPE OF LVCRECE.

Nor shall he smile at thee in secret thought,
Nor laugh with his companions at thy state,
But thou shalt know thy intrest was not bought
Basely with gold, but stolne from foorth thy gate.
For me I am the mistresse of my fate,
   And with my trespasse neuer will dispence,
   Till life to death acquit my forst offence.

I will not poyson thee with my attaint,
Nor fold my fault in cleanly coin'd excuses,
My sable ground of sinne I will not paint,
To hide the truth of this false nights abuses.
My tongue shall vtter all, mine eyes like sluces,
   As from a mountaine spring that feeds a dale,
   Shal gush pure streams to purge my impure tale.

By this lamenting Philomele had ended
The well-tun'd warble of her nightly sorrow,
And solemne night with slow sad gate descended
To ouglie Hell, when loe the blushing morrow
Lends light to all faire eyes that light will borrow.
   But cloudie LVCRECE shames her selfe to see,
   And therefore still in night would cloistred be.

                    Reuealing

THE RAPE OF LVCRECE.

Reuealing day through euery crannie ſpies,
And ſeems to point her out where ſhe ſits weeping,
To whom ſhee ſobbing ſpeakes, ô eye of eyes, (ping,
VVhy pry'ſt thou throgh my window? leaue thy pee-
Mock with thy tickling beams, eies that are ſleeping;
   Brand not my forehead with thy percing light,
   For day hath nought to do what's done by night.

Thus cauils ſhee with eueriē thing ſhee ſees,
True griefe is fond and teſtie as a childe,
VVho wayward once, his mood with naught agrees,
Old woes, not infant ſorrowes beare them milde,
Continuance tames the one, the other wilde,
   Like an vnpractiz'd ſwimmer plunging ſtill,
   VVith too much labour drowns for want of skill.

So ſhee deepe drenched in a Sea of care,
Holds diſputation with ech thing ſhee vewes,
And to her ſelfe all ſorrow doth compare,
No obiect but her paſſions ſtrength renewes :
And as one ſhiftes another ſtraight inſewes,
   Somtime her griefe is dumbe and hath no words,
   Sometime tis mad and too much talke affords.

H 3

THE RAPE OF LVCRECE.

The little birds that tune their mornings ioy,
Make her mones mad, with their sweet melodie,
"For mirth doth search the bottome of annoy,
" Sad foules are slaine in merrie companie,
" Griefe best is pleaf'd with griefes focietie ;
   " True forrow then is feelinglie suffiz'd,
    " VVhen with like femblance it is fimpathiz'd.

" Tis double death to drowne in ken of fhore,
" He ten times pines,that pines beholding food,
" To fee the falue doth make the wound ake more:
" Great griefe greeues most at that wold do it good;
" Deepe woes rowle forward like a gentle flood,
   VVho being stopt,the bouding banks oreflowes,
   Griefe dallied with, nor law, nor limit knowes.

You mocking Birds(quoth fhe)your tunes intombe
VVithin your hollow fwelling feathered breasts,
And in my hearing be you mute and dumbe,
My restlesse difcord loues no stops nor rests :
" A woefull Hostesse brookes not merrie guests.
   Ralifh your nimble notes to pleasing eares,
    "Distres likes dups whe time is kept with teares.

          H 3   Come

THE RAPE OF LVCRECE.

Come Philomele that fing'ft of rauifhment,
Make thy fad groue in my difheueld heare,
As the danke earth weepes at thy languifhment:
So I at each fad ftraine, will ftraine a teare,
And with deepe grones the Diapafon beare:
  For burthen-wife ile hum on TARQVIN ftill,
  VVhile thou on TEREVS defcants better skill.

And whiles againft a thorne thou bear'ft thy part,
To keepe thy fharpe woes waking, wretched I
To imitate thee well, againft my heart
VVill fixe a fharpe knife to affright mine eye,
VVho if it winke fhall thereon fall and die.
  Thefe meanes as frets vpon an inftrument,
  Shal tune our heart-ftrings to true languifhment.

And for poore bird thou fing'ft not in the day,
As fhaming anie eye fhould thee behold;
Some darke deepe defert feated from the way,
That knowes not parching heat, nor freezing cold
VVill wee find out: and there we will vnfold
  To creatures ftern, fad tunes to change their kinds,
  Since mē proue beafts, let beafts bear gētle minds.

THE RAPE OF LVCRECE.

As the poore frighted Deare that ftands at gaze,
VVildly determining which way to flie,
Or one incompaft with a winding maze,
That cannot tread the way out readilie:
So with her felfe is fhee in mutinie,
 To liue or die which of the twaine were better,
 VVhen life is fham'd and death reproches detter.

To kill my felfe, quoth fhee, alacke what were it,
But with my body my poore foules pollufion?
They that loofe halfe with greater patience beare it,
Then they whofe whole is fwallowed in confufion.
That mother tries a mercileffe conclufion,
 VVho hauing two fweet babes, when death takes
 VVill flay the other, and be nurfe to none. (one,

My bodie or my foule which was the dearer?
VVhen the one pure, the other made deuine,
VVhofe loue of eyther to my felfe was nearer?
VVhen both were kept for Heauen and COLATINE:
Ay me, the Barke pild from the loftie Pine,
 His leaues will wither, and his fap decay,
 So muft my foule her barke being pild away.

          Her

THE RAPE OF LVCRECE.

Her house is sackt, her quiet interrupted,
Her mansion batterd by the enemie,
Her sacred temple spotted, spoild, corrupted,
Groslie ingirt with daring infamie.
Then let it not be cald impietie,
 If in this blemisht fort I make some hole,
 Through which I may conuay this troubled soule.

Yet die I will not, till my COLATINE
Haue heard the cause of my vntimelie death,
That he may vow in that sad houre of mine,
Reuenge on him that made me stop my breath,
My stained bloud to TARQVIN ile bequeath,
 VVhich by him tainted, shall for him be spent,
 And as his due writ in my testament.

My Honor ile bequeath vnto the knife
That wounds my bodie so dishonored,
Tis Honor to depriue dishonord life,
The one will liue, the other being dead.
So of shames ashes shall my Fame be bred,
 For in my death I murther shamefull scorne,
 My shame so dead, mine honor is new borne.

I

THE RAPE OF LVCRECE.

Deare Lord of that deare iewell I haue loſt,
VVhat legacie ſhall I bequeath to thee?
My reſolution loue ſhall be thy boſt,
By whoſe example thou reueng'd mayſt be.
How TARQVIN muſt be vſd, read it in me,
    My ſelfe thy friend will kill my ſelfe thy fo,
    And for my ſake ſerue thou falſe TARQVIN ſo.

This briefe abridgement of my will I make,
My ſoule and bodie to the skies and ground:
My reſolution Husband doe thou take,
Mine Honor be the knifes that makes my wound,
My ſhame be his that did my Fame confound;
    And all my Fame that liues disburſed be,
    To thoſe that liue and thinke no ſhame of me.

Thou COLATINE ſhalt ouerſee this will,
How was I ouerſeene that thou ſhalt ſee it?
My bloud ſhall waſh the ſclander of mine ill,
My liues foule deed my lifes faire end ſhall free it.
Faint not faint heart, but ſtoutlie ſay ſo be it,
    Yeeld to my hand, my hand ſhall conquer thee,
    Thou dead, both die, and both ſhall victors be.
                                            This

THE RAPE OF LVCRECE.

This plot of death when sadlie shee had layd,
And wip't the brinish pearle from her bright eies,
VVith vntun'd tongue shee hoarslie cals her mayd,
VVhose swift obedience to her mistresse hies.
"For fleet-wing'd duetie with thoghts feathers flies,
   Poore LVCRECE cheeks vnto her maid seem so,
   As winter meads when sun doth melt their snow.

Her mistresse shee doth giue demure good morrow,
VVith soft slow-tongue, true marke of modestie,
And sorts a sad looke to her Ladies sorrow,
(For why her face wore sorrowes liuerie.)
But durst not aske of her audaciouslie,
   VVhy her two suns were clowd ecclipsed so,
   Nor why her faire cheeks ouer-washt with woe.

But as the earth doth weepe the Sun being set,
Each flowre moistned like a melting eye:
Euen so the maid with swelling drops gan wet
Her circled eien inforst, by simpathie
Of those faire Suns set in her mistresse skie,
   VVho in a salt wau'd Ocean quench their light,
   VVhich makes the maid weep like the dewy night.

I 2

THE RAPE OF LVCRECE.

A prettie while thefe prettie creatures ſtand,
Like Iuorie conduits corall ceſterns filling:
One iuſtlie weepes, the other takes in hand
No cauſe, but companie of her drops ſpilling.
Their gentle ſex to weepe are often willing,
   Greeuing themſelues to geſſe at others ſmarts,
   And thē they drown their eies, or break their harts.

For men haue marble, women waxen mindes,
And therefore are they form'd as marble will,
The weake oppreſt, th'impreſſion of ſtrange kindes
Is form'd in them by force, by fraud, or skill.
Then call them not the Authors of their ill,
   No more then waxe ſhall be accounted euill,
   VVherein is ſtampt the ſemblance of a Deuill.

Their ſmoothneſſe, like a goodly champaine plaine,
Laies open all the little wormes that creepe,
In men as in a rough-growne groue remaine.
Caue keeping euils that obſcurely ſleepe.
Through chriſtall wals ech little mote will peepe,
   Though mē cā couer crimes with bold ſtern looks,
   Poore womens faces are their owne faults books.

                              No

THE RAPE OF LVCRECE.

No man inueigh againſt the withered flowre,
But chide rough winter that the flowre hath kild,
Not that deuour'd, but that which doth deuour
Is worthie blame, ô let it not be hild
Poore womens faults, that they are ſo fulfild
 VVith mens abuſes, thoſe proud Lords to blame,
 Make weak-made womē tenants to their ſhame.

The preſident whereof in LVCRECE view,
Aſſail'd by night with circumſtances ſtrong
Of preſent death, and ſhame that might inſue.
By that her death to do her husband wrong,
Such danger to reſiſtance did belong:
 That dying feare through all her bodie ſpred,
 And who cannot abuſe a bodie dead ?

By this milde patience bid faire LVCRECE ſpeake,
To the poore counterfaite of her complayning,
My girle, quoth ſhee, on what occaſion breake
Thoſe tears frō thee, that downe thy cheeks are raig-
If thou doſt weepe for griefe of my ſuſtaining: (ning?
 Know gentle wench it ſmall auailes my mood,
 If tears could help, mine own would do me good.

I 3

THE RAPE OF LVCRECE.

But tell me girle, when went (and there shee staide,
Till after a deepe grone) TARQVIN from hence,
Madame ere I was vp (repli'd the maide,)
The more to blame my sluggard negligence.
Yet with the fault I thus farre can dispence:
  My selfe was stirring ere the breake of day,
  And ere I rose was TARQVIN gone away.

But Lady, if your maide may be so bold,
Shee would request to know your heauinesse:
(O peace quoth LVCRECE) if it should be told,
The repetition cannot make it lesse:
For more it is, then I can well expresse,
  And that deepe torture may be cal'd a Hell,
  VVhen more is felt then one hath power to tell.

Go get mee hither paper, inke, and pen,
Yet saue that labour, for I haue them heare,
(VVhat should I say) one of my husbands men
Bid thou be readie, by and by, to beare
A letter to my Lord, my Loue, my Deare,
  Bid him with speede prepare to carrie it,
  The cause craues hast, and it will soone be writ.

Her

THE RAPE OF LVCRECE.

Her maide is gone, and shee prepares to write,
First houering ore the paper with her quill :
Conceipt and griefe an eager combat fight,
VVhat wit sets downe is blotted straight with will,
This is too curious good, this blunt and ill,
    Much like a presse of people at a dore,
    Throng her inuentions which shall go before.

At last shee thus begins : thou worthie Lord,
Of that vnworthie wife that greeteth thee,
Health to thy person, next, vouchsafe t'afford
(If euer loue, thy LVCRECE thou wilt see,)
Some present speed, to come and visite me:
    So I commend me, from our house in griefe,
    My woes are tedious, though my words are briefe.

Here folds shee vp the tenure of her woe,
Her certaine sorrow writ vncertainely,
By this short Cedule COLATINE may know
Her griefe, but not her griefes true quality,
Shee dares not thereof make discouery,
    Lest he should hold it her own grosse abuse,
    Ere she with bloud had stain'd her stain'd excuse.

THE RAPE OF LVCRECE.

Besides the life and feeling of her passion,
Shee hoords to spend, when he is by to heare her,
VVhen sighs,&grones,&tears may grace the fashiō
Of her disgrace, the better so to cleare her
From that suspiciō which the world might bear her.
   To shun this blot, shee would not blot the letter
   VVith words,till action might becom thē better.

To see sad sights,moues more then heare them told,
For then the eye interpretes to the eare
The heauie motion that it doth behold,
VVhen euerie part, a part of woe doth beare.
Tis but a part of sorrow that we heare,
   Deep-sounds make lesser noise thē shallow foords,
   And sorrow ebs,being blown with wind of words.

Her letter now is seal'd, and on it writ
At ARDEA to my Lord with more then hast,
The Post attends, and shee deliuers it,
Charging the sowr-fac'd groome, to high as fast
As lagging fowles before the Northerne blast,
   Speed more then speed,but dul & slow she deems,
   Extremity still vrgeth such extremes.

                        The

THE RAPE OF LVCRECE.

The homelie villaine curſies to her low,
And bluſhing on her with a ſtedfaſt eye,
Receaues the ſcroll without or yea or no,
And forth with baſhfull innocence doth hie.
But they whoſe guilt within their boſomes lie,
   Imagine euerie eye beholds their blame,
   For LVCRECE thought, he bluſht to ſee her ſhame.

VVhen ſeelie Groome (God wot) it was defect
Of ſpirite, life, and bold audacitie,
Such harmleſſe creatures haue a true reſpect
To talke in deeds, while others ſauçilie
Promiſe more ſpeed, but do it leyſurelie.
   Euen ſo this patterne of the worne-out age,
   Pawn'd honeſt looks, but laid no words to gage.

His kindled duetie kindled her miſtruſt,
That two red fires in both their faces blazed,
Shee thought he bluſht, as knowing TARQVINS luſt,
And bluſhing with him, wiſtlie on him gazed,
Her earneſt eye did make him more amazed.
   The more ſhee ſaw the bloud his cheeks repleniſh,
   The more ſhe thought he ſpied in her ſom blemiſh.

K

THE RAPE OF LVCRECE.

But long fhee thinkes till he returne againe,
And yet the dutious vaffall fcarce is gone,
The wearie time fhee cannot entertaine,
For now tis ftale to figh, to weepe, and grone,
So woe hath wearied woe, mone tired mone,
    That fhee her plaints a little while doth ftay,
    Pawfing for meaus to mourne fome newer way.

At laft fhee cals to mind where hangs a peece
Of skilfull painting, made for PRIAMS Troy,
Before the which is drawn the power of Greece,
For HELENS rape, the Cittie to deftroy,
Threatning cloud-kiffing ILLION with annoy,
    VVhich the conceipted Painter drew fo prowd,
    As Heauen (it feem'd) to kiffe the turrets bow'd.

A thoufand lamentable obiects there,
In fcorne of Nature, Art gaue liueleffe life,
Many a dry drop feem'd a weeping teare,
Shed for the flaughtred husband by the wife.
The red bloud reek'd to fhew the Painters ftrife,
    And dying eyes gleem'd forth their afhie lights,
    Like dying coales burnt out in tedious nights.
                          There

THE RAPE OF LVCRECE.

There might you fee the labouring Pyoner
Begrim'd with fweat, and fmeared all with duft,
And from the towres of Troy, there would appeare
The verie eyes of men through loop-holes thruft,
Gazing vppon the Greekes with little luft,
 Such fweet obferuance in this worke was had,
 That one might fee thofe farre of eyes looke fad.

In great commaunders, Grace, and Maieftie,
You might behold triumphing in their faces,
In youth quick-bearing and dexteritie,
And here and there the Painter interlaces
Pale cowards marching on with trembling paces.
 VVhich hartleffe peafaunts did fo wel refemble,
 That one would fwear he faw them quake & treble.

In AIAX and VLYSSES, ô what Art
Of Phifiognomy might one behold!
The face of eyther cypher'd eythers heart,
Their face, their manners moft expreflie told,
In AIAX eyes blunt rage and rigour rold,
 But the mild glance that flie VLYSSES lent,
 Shewed deepe regard and fmiling gouernment.

K 2

129

THE RAPE OF LVCRECE.

There pleading might you see graue NESTOR stand,
As'twere incouraging the Greekes to fight,
Making such sober action with his hand,
That it beguild attention, charm'd the sight,
In speech it seemd his beard, all siluer white,
 VVag'd vp and downe, and from his lips did flie,
 Thin winding breath which purl'd vp to the skie.

About him were a presse of gaping faces,
VVhich seem'd to swallow vp his sound aduice,
All ioyntlie listning, but with seuerall graces,
As if some Marmaide did their eares intice,
Some high, some low, the Painter was so nice.
 The scalpes of manie almost hid behind,
 To iump vp higher seem'd to mocke the mind.

Here one mans hand leand on anothers head,
His nose being shadowed by his neighbours eare,
Here one being throng'd, bears back all boln, & red,
Another smotherd, seemes to pelt and sweare,
And in their rage such signes of rage they beare,
 As but for losse of NESTORS golden words,
 It seem'd they would debate with angrie swords.

           For

THE RAPE OF LVCRECE

For much imaginarie worke was there,
Conceipt deceitfull, ſo compact ſo kinde,
That for ACHILLES image ſtood his ſpeare
Grip't in an Armed hand,himſelfe behind
VVas left vnſeene, ſaue to the eye of mind,
   A hand, a foote, a face, a leg, a head
    Stood for the whole to be imagined.

And from the wals of ſtrong beſieged TROY, (field,
VVhen their braue hope, bold HECTOR march'd to
Stood manie Troian mothers ſharing ioy,
To ſee their youthfull ſons bright weapons wield,
And to their hope they ſuch odde action yeeld,
   That through their light ioy ſeemed to appeare,
    (Like bright things ſtaind) a kind of heauie feare.

And from the ſtrond of DARDAN where they fought,
To SIMOIS reedie bankes the red bloud ran,
VVhoſe waues to imitate the battaile ſought
VVith ſwelling ridges, and their rankes began
To breake vppon the galled ſhore, and than
   Retire againe, till meeting greater ranckes
    They ioine, & ſhoot their fome at SIMOIS bancks.

K 3

THE RAPE OF LVCRECE.

To this well painted peece is LVCRECE come,
To find a face where all diftreffe is fteld,
Manie fhee fees, where cares haue carued fome,
But none where all diftreffe and dolor dweld,
Till fhee difpayring HECVBA beheld,
    Staring on PRIAMS wounds with her old eyes,
    VVhich bleeding vnder PIRRHVS proud foot lies.

In her the Painter had anathomiz'd
Times ruine, beauties wracke, and grim cares raign,
Her cheeks with chops and wrincles were difguiz'd,
Of what fhee was, no femblance did remaine:
Her blew bloud chang'd to blacke in euerie vaine,
    VVanting the fpring, that thofe fhrunke pipes had
    Shew'd life imprifon'd in a bodie dead. (fed,

On this fad fhadow LVCRECE fpends her eyes,
And fhapes her forrow to the Beldames woes,
VVho nothing wants to anfwer her but cries,
And bitter words to ban her cruell Foes:
The Painter was no God to lend her thofe,
    And therefore LVCRECE fwears he did her wrong,
    To giue her fo much griefe, and not a tong.

                                    Poore

THE RAPE OF LVCRECE.

Poore Inſtrument (queth ſhee) without a ſound,
Ile tune thy woes with my lamenting tongue,
And drop ſweet Balme in PRIAMS painted wound,
And raile on PIRRHVS that hath done him wrong;
And with my tears quench Troy that burns ſo long;
 And with my knife ſcratch out the angrie eyes,
 Of all the Greekes that are thine enemies.

Shew me the ſtrumpet that began this ſtur,
That with my nailes her beautie I may teare:
Thy heat of luſt fond PARIS did incur
This lode of wrath, that burning Troy doth beare;
Thy eye kindled the fire that burneth here,
 And here in Troy for treſpaſſe of thine eye,
 The Sire, the ſonne, the Dame and daughter die.

VVhy ſhould the priuate pleaſure of ſome one
Become the publicke plague of manie moe?
Let ſinne alone committed, light alone
Vppon his head that hath tranſgreſſed ſo.
Let guiltleſſe ſoules be freed from guilty woe,
 For ones offence why ſhould ſo many fall?
 To plague a priuate ſinne in generall.

THE RAPE OF LVCRECE.

Lo here weeps Hecvba, here Priam dies,
Here manly Hector faints, here Troylvs founds,
Here friend by friend in bloudie channel lies:
And friend to friend giues vnaduifed wounds,
And one mans luft thefe manie liues confounds.
 Had doting Priam checkt his fons defire,
  Troy had bin bright with Fame, & not with fire.

Here feelingly fhe weeps Troyes painted woes,
For forrow, like a heauie hanging Bell,
Once fet on ringing, with his own waight goes,
Then little ftrength rings out the dolefull knell,
So Lvcrece fet a worke, fad tales doth tell
 To pencel'd penfiuenes, & colour'd forrow, (row,
  She lends them words, & fhe their looks doth bor-

Shee throwes her eyes about the painting round,
And who fhee finds forlorne, fhee doth lament:
At laft fhee fees a wretched image bound,
That piteous lookes, to Phrygian fheapheards lent,
His face though full of cares, yet fhew'd content,
 Onward to Troy with the blunt fwains he goes,
  So mild that patience feem'd to fcorne his woes.
          In

THE RAPE OF LVCRECE.

In him the Painter labour'd with his skill
To hide deceipt, and giue the harmlesse show
An humble gate, calme looks, eyes wayling still,
A brow vnbent that seem'd to welcome wo,
Cheeks neither red, nor pale, but mingled so,
    That blushing red, no guiltie instance gaue,
    Nor ashie pale, the feare that false hearts haue.

But like a constant and confi med Deuill,
He entertain'd a show, so seeming iust,
And therein so ensconc't his secret euill,
That Iealousie it selfe could not mistrust,
False creeping Craft, and Periurie should thrust
    Into so bright a daie, such blackfac'd storms,
    Or blot with Hell-born sin such Saint-like forms.

The well-skil'd workman this milde Image drew
For periur'd Sinon, whose inchaunting storie
The credulous old Priam after slew.
VVhose words like wild fire burnt the shining glorie
Of rich-built Illion, that the skies were sorie,
    And little stars shot from their fixed places,
    VVhe their glas fel, wherin they view'd their faces.

L

THE RAPE OF LVCRECE.

This picture shee aduisedly perus'd,
And chid the Painter for his wondrous skill:
Saying,some shape in S IN O N S was abus'd,
So faire a forme lodg'd not a mind so ill,
And still on him shee gaz'd, and gazing still,
    Such signes of truth in his plaine face shee spied,
    That shee concludes, the Picture was belied.

It cannot be (quoth she) that so much guile,
(Shee would haue said) can lurke in such a looke:
But T A R Q V I N S shape,came in her mind the while,
And from her tongue, can lurk,from cannot, tooke
It cannot be, shee in that sence forsooke,
    And turn'd it thus, it cannot be I find,
    But such a face should beare a wicked mind.

For euen as subtill S I N O N here is painted,
So sober sad, so wearie, and so milde,
(As if with griefe or trauaile he had fainted)
To me came T A R Q V I N armed to beguild
VVith outward honestie, but yet defild
    VVith inward vice,as P R I A M him did cherish:
    So did I T A R Q V I N, so my Troy did perish.

                        Looke

THE RAPE OF LVCRECE.

Looke looke how liſtning P R I A M wets his eyes,
To ſee thoſe borrowed teares that S I N O N ſheeds,
P R I A M why art thou old, and yet not wiſe?
For euerie teare he fals a Troian bleeds:
His eye drops fire, no water thence proceeds,
  Thoſe roūd clear pearls of his that moue thy pitty,
  Are bals of quenchleſſe fire to burne thy Citty.

Such Deuils ſteale effects from lightleſſe Hell,
For S I N O N in his fire doth quake with cold,
And in that cold hot burning fire doth dwell,
Theſe contraries ſuch vnitie do hold,
Only to flatter fooles, and make them bold,
  So P R I A M S truſt falſe S I N O N S teares doth flatter,
  That he finds means to burne his Troy with water.

Here all inrag'd ſuch paſſion her aſſailes,
That patience is quite beaten from her breaſt,
Shee tears the ſenceleſſe S I N O N with her nailes,
Comparing him to that vnhappie gueſt,
VVhoſe deede hath made herſelfe, herſelfe deteſt,
  At laſt ſhee ſmilingly with this giues ore,
  Foole fool, quoth ſhe, his wounds wil not be ſore.

L 2

137

THE RAPE OF LVCRECE.

Thus ebs and flowes the currant of her forrow,
And time doth wearie time with her complayning,
Shee looks for night, & then fhee longs for morrow,
And both fhee thinks too long with her remayning.
Short time feems long, in forrowes fharp fuftayning,
 Though wo be heauie, yet it feldome fleepes,
 And they that watch, fee time, how flow it creeps.

VVhich all this time hath ouerflipt her thought,
That fhee with painted Images hath fpent,
Being from the feeling of her own griefe brought,
By deepe furmife of others detriment,
Loofing her woes in fhews of difcontent:
 It eafeth fome, though none it euer cured,
 To thinke their dolour others haue endured.

But now the mindfull Meffenger come backe,
Brings home his Lord and other companie,
VVho finds his LVCRECE clad in mourning black,
And round about her teare-diftained eye
Blew circles ftream'd, like Rain-bows in the skie.
 Thefe watergalls in her dim Element,
 Foretell new ftormes to thofe alreadie fpent.
         VVhich

THE RAPE OF LVCRECE.

VVhich when her sad beholding husband saw,
Amazedlie in her sad face he stares:
Her eyes though sod in tears look'd red and raw,
Her liuelie colour kil'd with deadlie cares,
He hath no power to aske her how shee fares,
    Both stood like old acquaintance in a trance,
    Met far from home, wondring ech others chance.

At last he takes her by the bloudlesse hand,
And thus begins: what vncouth ill euent
Hath thee befalne, that thou dost trembling stand?
Sweet loue what spite hath thy faire colour spent?
VVhy art thou thus attir'd in discontent?
    Vnmaske deare deare, this moodie heauinesse,
    And tell thy griefe, that we may giue redresse.

Three times with sighes shee giues her sorrow fire,
Ere once shee can discharge one word of woe:
At length addrest to answer his desire,
Shee modestlie prepares, to let them know
Her Honor is tane prisoner by the Foe,
    VVhile COLATINE and his consorted Lords,
    VVith sad attention long to heare her words.

L 3

139

THE RAPE OF LVCRECE.

And now this pale Swan in her watrie neſt,
Begins theſad Dirge of her certaine ending,
Few words (quoth ſhee) ſhall fit the treſpaſſe beſt,
VVhere no excuſe can giue the fault amending.
In me moe woes then words are now depending,
   And my laments would be drawn out too long,
   To tell them all with one poore tired tong.

Then be this all the taske it hath to ſay,
Deare husband in the intereſt of thy bed
A ſtranger came, and on that pillow lay,
VVhere thou waſt wont to reſt thy wearie head,
And what wrong elſe may be imagined,
   By foule inforcement might be done to me,
   From that (alas) thy LVCRECE is not free.

For in the dreadfull dead of darke midnight,
VVith ſhining Fauchion in my chamber came
A creeping creature with a flaming light,
And ſoftly cried, awake thou Romaine Dame,
And entertaine my loue, elſe laſting ſhame
   On thee and thine this night I will inflict,
   If thou my loues deſire do contradict.

                          For

THE RAPE OF LVCRECE.

For fome hard fauour'd Groome of thine, quoth he,
Vnleffe thou yoke thy liking to my will
Ile murther ftraight, and then ile flaughter thee,
And fweare I found you where you did fulfill
The lothfome act of Luft, and fo did kill
    The lechors in their deed, this Act will be
    My Fame, and thy perpetuall infamy.

VVith this I did begin to ftart and cry,
And then againft my heart he fet his fword,
Swearing, vnleffe I tooke all patiently,
I fhould not liue to fpeake another word.
So fhould my fhame ftill reft vpon record,
    And neuer be forgot in mightie Roome
    Th'adulterat death of LVCRECE, and her Groome.

Mine enemy was ftrong, my poore felfe weake,
(And farre the weaker with fo ftrong a feare)
My bloudie Iudge forbod my tongue to fpeake,
No rightfull plea might plead for Iuftice there.
His fcarlet Luft came euidence to fweare
    That my poore beautie had purloin'd his eyes,
    And when the Iudge is rob'd, the prifoner dies.

THE RAPE OF LVCRECE.

O teach me how to make mine owne excuse,
Or (at the least) this refuge let me finde,
Though my grosse bloud be staind with this abuse,
Immaculate, and spotlesse is my mind,
That was not forc'd, that neuer was inclind
  To accessarie yeeldings, but still pure
  Doth in her poyson'd closet yet endure.

Lo heare the hopelesse Marchant of this losse,
VVith head declin'd, and voice dam'd vp with wo,
VVith sad set eyes and wretched armes acrosse,
From lips new waxen pale, begins to blow
The griefe away, that stops his answer so.
  But wretched as he is he striues in vaine,
  VVhat he breaths out, his breath drinks vp again.

As through an Arch, the violent roaring tide,
Outruns the eye that doth behold his hast:
Yet in the Edie boundeth in his pride,
Backe to the strait that forst him on so fast:
In rage sent out, recald in rage being past,
  Euen so his sighes, his sorrowes make a saw,
  To push griefe on, and back the same grief draw.
                    VVhich

THE RAPE OF LVCRECE.

VVhich ſpeechleſſe woe of his poore ſhe attendeth,
And his vntimelie frenzie thus awaketh,
Deare Lord, thy ſorrow to my ſorrow lendeth
Another power, no floud by raining ſlaketh,
My woe too ſencible thy paſſion maketh
   More feeling painfull, let it than ſuffice
   To drowne on woe, one paire of weeping eyes.

And for my ſake when I might charme thee ſo,
For ſhee that was thy LVCRECE, now attend me,
Be ſodainelie reuenged on my Foe.
Thine, mine, his own, ſuppoſe thou doſt defend me
From what is paſt, the helpe that thou ſhalt lend me
   Comes all too late, yet let the Traytor die,
   "For ſparing Iuſtice feeds iniquitie.

But ere I name him, you faire Lords, quoth ſhee,
(Speaking to thoſe that came with COLATINE)
Shall plight your Honourable faiths to me,
VVith ſwift purſuit to venge this wrong of mine,
For'tis a meritorious faire deſigne,
   To chaſe iniuſtice with reuengefull armes,
   Knights by their oaths ſhould right poore Ladies
              M   (harmes.

THE RAPE OF LVCRECE.

At this requeſt, with noble diſpoſition,
Each preſent Lord began to promiſe aide,
As bound in Knighthood to her impoſition,
Longing to heare the hatefull Foe bewraide.
But ſhee that yet her ſad taske hath not ſaid,
   The proteſtation ſtops, ô ſpeake quoth ſhee,
   How may this forced ſtaine be wip'd from me?

VVhat is the qualitie of my offence
Being conſtrayn'd with dreadfull circumſtance?
May my pure mind with the fowle act diſpence
My low declined Honor to aduance?
May anie termes acquit me from this chance?
   The poyſoned fountaine cleares it ſelfe againe,
   And why not I from this compelled ſtaine?

VVith this they all at once began to ſaie,
Her bodies ſtaine, her mind vntainted cleares,
VVhile with a ioyleſſe ſmile, ſhee turnes awaie
The face, that map which deepe impreſſion beares
Of hard misfortune, caru'd it in with tears.
   No no, quoth ſhee, no Dame hereafter liuing,
   By my excuſe ſhall claime excuſes giuing.
                        Here

THE RAPE OF LVCRECE.

Here with a figh as if her heart would breake,
Shee throwes forth TARQVINS name:he he, fhe faies,
But more then he,her poore tong could not fpeake,
Till after manie accents and delaies,
Vntimelie breathings, ficke and fhort affaies,
 Shee vtters this, he he faire Lords, tis he
 That guides this hand to giue this wound to me.

Euen here fhe fheathed in her harmleffe breaft
A harmfull knife, that thence her foule vnfheathed,
That blow did baile it from the deepe vnreft
Of that polluted prifon, where it breathed:
Her contrite fighes vnto the clouds bequeathed
 Her winged fprite, & through her wou̅ds doth flie
 Liues lafting date, from cancel'd deftinie.

Stone ftill, aftonifht with this deadlie deed,
Stood COLATINE, and all his Lordly crew,
Till LVCRECE Father that beholds her bleed,
Himfelfe, on her felfe-flaughtred bodie threw,
And from the purple fountaine BRVTVS drew
 The murdrous knife, and as it left the place,
 Her bloud in poore reuenge, held it in chafe.

M 2

THE RAPE OF LVCRECE.

And bubling from her breſt, it doth deuide
In two ſlow riuers, that the crimſon bloud
Circles her bodie in on euerie ſide,
VVho like a late ſack't Iland vaſtlie ſtood
Bare and vnpeopled, in this fearfull flood.
  Some of her bloud ſtill pure and red remain'd,
   And ſom look'd black, & that falſe TARQVIN ſtain'd.

About the mourning and congealed face
Of that blacke bloud, a watrie rigoll goes,
VVhich ſeemes to weep vpon the tainted place,
And euer ſince as pittying LVCRECE woes,
Corrupted bloud, ſome waterie token ſhowes,
  And bloud vntainted, ſtill doth red abide,
   Bluſhing at that which is ſo putrified.

Daughter, deare daughter, old LVCRETIVS cries,
That life was mine which thou haſt here depriued,
If in the childe the fathers image lies,
VVhere ſhall I liue now LVCRECE is vnliued?
Thou waſt not to this end from me deriued.
  If children prædeceaſe progenitours,
   VVe are their offspring and they none of ours.

                         Poore

146

THE RAPE OF LVCRECE.

Poore broken glaſſe, I often did behold
In thy ſweet ſemblance, my old age new borne,
But now that faire freſh mirror dim and old
Shewes me a bare bon'd death by time out-worne,
O from thy cheekes my image thou haſt torne,
   And ſhiuerd all the beautie of my glaſſe,
   That I no more can ſee what once I was.

O time ceaſe thou thy courſe and laſt no longer,
If they ſurceaſe to be that ſhould ſuruiue :
Shall rotten death make conqueſt of the ſtronger,
And leaue the foultring feeble ſoules aliue?
The old Bees die, the young poſſeſſe their hiue,
   Then liue ſweet L V C R E C E, liue againe and ſee
   Thy father die, and not thy father thee.

By this ſtarts C O L A T I N E as from a dreame,
And bids L V C R E C I V S giue his ſorrow place,
And then in key-cold L V C R E C E bleeding ſtreame
He fals, and bathes the pale feare in his face,
And counterfaits to die with her a ſpace,
   Till manly ſhame bids him poſſeſſe his breath,
   And liue to be reuenged on her death.

M 3

THE RAPE OF LVCRECE.

The deepe vexation of his inward foule,
Hath feru'd a dumbe arreft vpon his tongue,
VVho mad that forrow fhould his vfe controll,
Or keepe him from heart-eafing words fo long,
Begins to talke, but through his lips do throng
  VVeake words, fo thick come in his poor harts aid,
   That no man could diftinguifh what he faid.

Yet fometime TARQVIN was pronounced plaine,
But through his teeth, as if the name he tore,
This windie tempeft, till it blow vp raine,
Held backe his forrowes tide, to make it more.
At laft it raines, and bufie windes giue ore,
  Then fonne and father weep with equall ftrife,
   VVho fhuld weep moft for daughter or for wife.

The one doth call her his, the other his,
Yet neither may poffeffe the claime they lay.
The father faies, fhee's mine, ô mine fhee is
Replies her husband, do not take away
My forrowes intereft, let no mourner fay
  He weepes for her, for fhee was onely mine,
   And onelie muft be wayl'd by COLATINE.

O,

THE RAPE OF LVCRECE.

O, quoth Lvcretivs, I did giue that life
VVhich fhee to earely and too late hath fpil'd.
VVoe woe, quoth Colatine, fhee was my wife,
I owed her, and tis mine that fhee hath kil'd.
My daughter and my wife with clamors fild
    The difperft aire, who holding Lvcrece life,
    Anfwer'd their cries, my daughter and my wife.

Brvtvs who pluck't the knife from Lvcrece fide,
Seeing fuch emulation in their woe,
Began to cloath his wit in ftate and pride,
Burying in Lvcrece wound his follies fhow,
He with the Romains was efteemed fo
    As feelie ieering idiots are with Kings,
    For fportiue words, and vttring foolifh things.

But now he throwes that fhallow habit by,
VVherein deepe pollicie did him difguife,
And arm'd his long hid wits aduifedlie,
To checke the teares in Colatinvs eies.
Thou wronged Lord of Rome, quoth he, arife,
    Let my vnfounded felfe fuppof'd a foole,
    Now fet thy long experienc't wit to fchoole.

THE RAPE OF LVCRECE.

VVhy COLATINE, is woe the cure for woe?
Do wounds helpe wounds, or griefe helpe greeuous
Is it reuenge to giue thy felfe a blow,   (deeds?
For his fowle Act, by whom thy faire wife bleeds?
Such childifh humor from weake minds proceeds,
 Thy wretched wife miftooke the matter fo,
 To flaie her felfe that fhould haue flaine her Foe.

Couragious Romaine, do not fteepe thy hart
In fuch relenting dew of Lamentations,
But kneele with me and helpe to beare thy part,
To rowfe our Romaine Gods with inuocations,
That they will fuffer thefe abhominations
 (Since Rome her felf in thē doth ftand difgraced,)
 By our ftrong arms frō forth her fair ftreets chaced.

Now by the Capitoll that we adore,
And by this chaft bloud fo vniuftlie ftained,
By heauens faire fun that breeds the fat earths ftore,
By all our countrey rights in Rome maintained,
And by chaft LVCRECE foule that late complained
 Her wrongs to vs, and by this bloudie knife,
 VVe will reuenge the death of this true wife.

        This

THE RAPE OF LVCRECE.

This fayd, he ftrooke his hand vpon his breaft,
And kift the fatall knife to end his vow:
And to his proteftation vrg'd the reft,
VVho wondring at him, did his words allow.
Then ioyntlie to the ground their knees they bow,
　　And that deepe vow which BRVTVS made before,
　　He doth againe repeat, and that they fwore.

VVhen they had fworne to this aduifed doome,
They did conclude to beare dead LVCRECE thence,
To fhew her bleeding bodie thorough Roome,
And fo to publifh TARQVINS fowle offence;
VVhich being done, with fpeedie diligence,
　　The Romaines plaufibly did giue confent,
　　To TARQVINS euerlafting banifhment.

N

FINIS.

THE PASSIONATE PILGRIM

SECOND EDITION

1599

The Huntington Library Copy

A

THE
PASSIONATE
PILGRIME.

By W. Shakespeare.

AT LONDON
Printed for W. Iaggard, and are
to be fold by W. Leake, at the Greyhound in Paules Churchyard.
1599.

WHen my Loue sweares that she is made of truth,
 I doe beleeue her (though I know she lies)
That she might thinke me some vntutor'd youth,
Vnskilfull in the worlds false forgeries.
Thus vainly thinking that she thinkes me young,
Although I know my yeares be past the best:
I smiling, credite her false speaking toung,
Outfacing faults in Loue, with loues ill rest.
But wherefore sayes my Loue that she is young?
And wherefore say not I, that I am old?
O, Loues best habite is a soothing toung,
And Age (in Loue) loues not to haue yeares told.
    Therfore Ile lye with Loue, and Loue with me,
    Since that our faults in Loue thus smother'd be.

A 3

TWo Loues I haue, of Comfort, and Defpaire,
That like two Spirits, do fuggeſt me ſtill:
My better Angell is a Man (right faire)
My worſer ſpirite a Woman (colour'd ill.)
To winne me ſoone to hell, my Female euill
Tempteth my better Angell from my ſide,
And would corrupt my Saint to be a Diuell,
Wooing his purity with her faire pride.
And whether that my Angell be turnde feend,
Suſpeſt I may (yet not directly tell:
For being both to me: both, to each friend,
I gheſſe one Angell in anothers hell:
    The truth I ſhall not know, but liue in doubt,
    Till my bad Angell fire my good one out.

III

Did not the heauenly Rhetorike of thine eie,
 Gainſt whom the world could not hold argumēt,
Perſwade my hart to this falſe periurie :
Vowes for thee broke deſerue not puniſhment.
A woman I forſwore : but I will proue
Thou being a Goddeſſe, I forſwore not thee :
My vow was earthly, thou a heauenly loue,
Thy grace being gainde, cures all diſgrace in me.
My vow was breath, and breath a vapor is,
Then thou faire Sun, that on this earth doth ſhine,
Exhale this vapor vow, in thee it is :
If broken, then it is no fault of mine.
  If by me broke, what foole is not ſo wiſe
  To breake an Oath, to win a Paradiſe ?

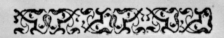

IV

SWeet Cytherea, sitting by a Brooke,
 With young Adonis, louely, fresh and greene,
Did court the Lad with many a louely looke,
Such lookes as none could looke but beauties queen,
She told him stories, to delight his eares :
She shew'd him fauors, to allure his eie :
To win his hart, she toucht him here and there,
Touches so soft still conquer chastitie.
But whether vnripe yeares did want conceit,
Or he refusde to take her figured proffer,
The tender nibler would not touch the bait,
But smile, and ieast, at euery gentle offer :
    Then fell she on her backe, faire queen, & toward
    He rose and ran away, ah foole too froward.

V

IF Loue make me forſworn, how ſhal I ſwere to loue?
O, neuer faith could hold, if not to beauty vowed:
Though to my ſelfe forſworn, to thee Ile conſtant proue,
thoſe thoghts to me like Okes, to thee like Oſiers bowed,
Studdy his byas leaues, and makes his booke thine eies,
where all thoſe pleaſures liue, that Art can comprehend:
It knowledge be the marke, to know thee ſhall ſuffice:
Wel learned is that toung that well can thee commend,
All ignorant that ſoule, that ſees thee without wonder,
Which is to me ſome praiſe, that I thy parts admyre:
Thine eye loues lightning ſeems, thy voice his dreadfull
which (not to anger bent) is muſick & ſweet fire(thunder
Celeſtiall as thou art, O, do not loue that wrong:
To ſing heauens praiſe, with ſuch an earthly toung.

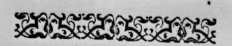

VI

SCarſe had the Sunne dride vp the deawy morne,
And ſcarſe the heard gone to the hedge for ſhade:
When Cytherea (all in Loue forlorne)
A longing tariance for Adonis made
Vnder an Oſyer growing by a brooke,
A brooke, where Adon vſde to coole his ſpleene:
Hot was the day, ſhe hotter that did looke
For his approch, that often there had beene.
Anon he comes, and throwes his Mantle by,
And ſtood ſtarke naked on the brookes greene brim:
The Sunne look't on the world with glorious eie,
Yet not ſo wiſtly, as this Queene on him:
   He ſpying her, bounſt in (whereas he ſtood)
   Oh I o v e (quoth ſhe) why was not I a flood?

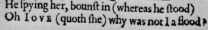

VII

FAire is my loue, but not so faire as fickle.
  Milde as a Doue, but neither true nor trustie,
Brighter then glasse, and yet as glasse is brittle,
Softer then waxe, and yet as Iron rusty :
  A lilly pale, with damaske die to grace her,
  None fairer, nor none falser to deface her.

Her lips to mine how often hath she ioyned,
Betweene each kisse her othes of true loue swearing:
How many tales to please me hath she coyned,
Dreading my loue, the losse whereof still fearing.
  Yet in the mids of all her pure protestings,
  Her faith, her othes, her teares, and all were iesting.

She burnt with loue, as straw with fire flameth,
She burnt out loue, as soone as straw out burneth:
She fram d the loue, and yet she foyl d the framing,
She bad loue last, and yet she fell a turning.
  Was this a louer, or a Letcher whether ?
  Bad in the best, though excellent in neither.
                    B

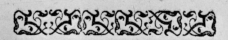

VIII

IF Muſicke and ſweet Poetrie agree,
As they muſt needs (the Siſter and the brother)
Then muſt the loue be great twixt thee and me,
Becauſe thou lou'ſt the one, and I the other.
Dowland to thee is deere, whoſe heauenly tuch
Vpon the Lute, dooth rauiſh humane ſenſe:
Spenſer to me, whoſe deepe Conceit is ſuch,
As paſsing all conceit, needs no defence.
Thou lou'ſt to heare the ſweet melodious ſound,
That Phœbus Lute (the Queene of Muſicke) makes;
And I in deepe Delight am chiefly drownd,
When as himſelfe to ſinging he betakes.
  One God is God of both (as Poets faine)
  One Knight loues Both, and both in thee remaine.

IX

FAire was the morne, when the faire Queene of Ioue,
 Paler for sorrow then her milke white Doue,
For Adons sake, a youngster proud and wilde,
Her stand she takes vpon a steepe vp hill.
Anon Adonis comes with horne and hounds,
She silly Queene, with more then loues good will,
Forbad the boy he should not passe those grounds,
Once (quoth she) did I see a faire sweet youth
Here in these brakes, deepe wounded with a Boare,
Deepe in the thigh a spectacle of ruth,
See in my thigh (quoth she) here was the sore,
 She shewed hers, he saw more wounds then one,
 And blushing fled, and left her all alone.

B 3

X

SWeet Rose, faire flower, vntimely pluckt, soon vaded,
Pluckt in the bud, and vaded in the spring:
Bright orient pearle, alacke too timely shaded,
Faire creature kilde too soon by Deaths sharpe sting:
    Like a greene plumbe that hangs vpon a tree:
    And fals (through winde) before the fall should be.

I weepe for thee, and yet no cause I haue,
For why: thou lefts me nothing in thy will·
And yet thou lefts me more then I did craue,
For why: I craued nothing of thee still:
    O yes (deare friend I pardon craue of thee,
    Thy discontent thou didst bequeath to me.

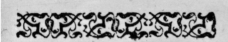

XI

VEnus with Adonis ſitting by her,
  Vnder a Mirtle ſhade began to wooe him,
She told the youngling how god Mars did trie her,
And as he fell to her, ſhe fell to him.
Euen thus (quoth ſhe) the warlike god embrac't me:
And then ſhe clipt Adonis in her armes :
Euen thus (quoth ſhe) the warlike god vnlaç't me,
As if the boy ſhould vſe like louing charmes :
Euen thus (quoth ſhe) he ſeized on my lippes,
And with her lips on his did act the ſeizure :
And as ſhe fetched breath, away he skips,
And would not take her meaning nor her pleaſure.
  Ah, that I had my Lady at this bay :
  To kiſſe and clip me till I run away.

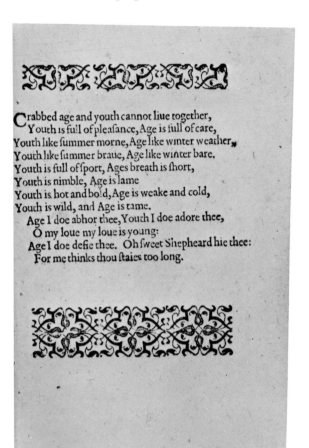

XII

Crabbed age and youth cannot liue together,
  Youth is full of pleasance, Age is full of care,
Youth like summer morne, Age like winter weather,
Youth like summer braue, Age like winter bare.
Youth is full of sport, Ages breath is short,
Youth is nimble, Age is lame
Youth is hot and bold, Age is weake and cold,
Youth is wild, and Age is tame.
  Age I doe abhor thee, Youth I doe adore thee,
    O my loue my loue is young:
  Age I doe defie thee. Oh sweet Shepheard hie thee:
    For me thinks thou staies too long.

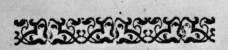

XIII

BEauty is but a vaine and doubtfull good,
A shining glosse, that vadeth sodainly,
A flower that dies, when first it gins to bud,
A brittle glasse, that s broken presently.
    A doubtfull good, a glosse, a glasse, a flower,
    Lost, vaded, broken, dead within an houre.

And as goods lost, are seld or neuer found,
As vaded glosse no rubbing will refresh :
As flowers dead, lie withered on the ground,
As broken glasse no symant can redresse.
    So beauty blemisht once, for euer lost,
    In spite of phisicke, painting, paine and cost.

XIV

Good night, good reſt, ah neither be my ſhare,
　She bad good night, that kept my reſt away,
And daſt me to a cabben hangde with care:
To deſcant on the doubts of my decay.
　Farewell (quoth ſhe) and come againe to morrow
　Fare well I could not, for I ſupt with ſorrow.

Yet at my parting ſweetly did ſhe ſmile,
In ſcorne or friendſhip, nill I conſter whether :
'Tmay be ſhe ioyd to ieaſt at my exile,
'Tmay be againe, to make me wander thither.
　Wander (a word) for ſhadowes like my ſelfe,
　As take the paine but cannot plucke the pelfe.

Lord

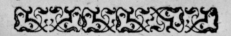

Lord how mine eies throw gazes to the Eaſt,
My hart doth charge the watch, the morning riſe
Doth ſcite each mouing ſcence from idle reſt,
Not daring truſt the office of mine eies.
　While Philomela ſits and ſings, I ſit and mark,
　And with her layes were tuned like the larke.

For ſhe doth welcome daylight with her ditte,
And driues away darke dreaming night:
The night ſo packt, I poſt vnto my pretty,
Hart hath his hope, and eies their wiſhed ſight,
　Sorrow changd to ſolace, and ſolace mixt with ſorrow,
　For why, ſhe ſight, and bad me come to morrow.

　　　　　　　C

Were I with her, the night would post too soone,
But now are minutes added to the houres:
To spite me now, ech minute seemes an houre,
Yet not for me, shine sun to succour flowers.
    Pack night, peep day, good day of night now borrov
    Short night to night, and length thy selfe to morrov

SONNETS

To sundry notes of Muficke.

AT LONDON
Printed for W. Iaggard, and are
to be fold by W. Leake, at the Greyhound in Paules Churchyard.
1599.

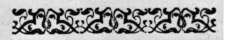

XV

IT was a Lordings daughter, the faireſt one of three
That liked of her maiſter, as well as well might be,
Till looking on an Engliſhman, the faireſt that eie coul
   Her fancie fell a turning.
Long was the combat doubtfull, that loue with loue did
To leaue the maiſter loueleſſe, or kill the gallant knight
To put in practiſe either, alas it was a ſpite
   Vnto the ſilly damſell.
But one muſt be refuſed, more mickle was the paine,
That nothing could be vſed, to turne them both to gai
For of the two the truſty knight was wounded with diſ
   Alas ſhe could not helpe it.
Thus art with armes contending, was victor of the day
Which by a gift of learning, did beare the maid away,
Then luſlaby the learned man hath got the Lady gay,
   For now my ſong is ended.

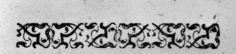

XVI

ON a day.(alacke the day)
  Loue whofe month was euer May·
Spied a bloffome paffing fair,
Playing in the wanton ayre,
Through the veluet leaues the wind
All vnfeene gan paffage find,
That the louer (ficke to death)
Wifht himfelfe the heauens breath,
Ayre (quoth he) thy cheekes may blowe
Ayre, would I might triumph fo
But (alas)my hand hath fworne,
Nere to plucke thee from thy throne,
Vow(alacke) for youth vnmeet,
Youth,fo apt to pluck a fweet,
Thou for whome Ioue would fweare,
Iuno but an Ethiope were
And deny hymfelfe for Ioue
Turning mortall for thy Loue.

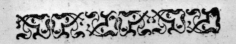

XVII

MY flocks feede not, my Ewes breed not,
My Rams speed not, all is amis:
Loue is dying, Faithes defying,
Harts nenying, causer of this,
All my merry Iigges are quite forgot,
All my Ladies loue is lost (god wot)
Where her faith was firmely fixt in loue,
There a nay is plac't without remoue.
One silly crosse, wrought all my losse,
O frowning fortune cursed fickle dame,
For now I see, inconstancy,
More in wowen then in men remaine.

In blacke morne I, all feares scorne I,
Loue hath forlorne me, liuing in thrall:
Hart is bleeding, all helpe needing,
O cruell speeding, fraughted with gall.
My shepheards pipe can sound no deale,
My weathers bell rings dolefull knell,
My curtaile dogge that wont to haue plaid,
Plaies not at all but seemes afraid.
  With sighes so deepe, procures to weepe,
  In howling wise, to see my dolefull plight,
  How sighes resound through hartles ground
  Like a thousand vanquisht men in blodie fight.

Cleare wels spring not, sweete birds sing not,
Greene plants bring not forth their die,
Heards stands weeping, flocks all sleeping,
Nimphes blacke peeping fearefully:
All our pleasure knowne to vs poore swaines:
All our merrie meetings on the plaines,
All our euening sport from vs is fled,
All our loue is lost, for loue is dead,
    Farewell sweet loue thy like nere was,
    For a sweet content the cause of all my woe,
    Poore Coridon must liue alone,
    Other helpe for him I see that there is none.

When as thine eye hath chose the Dame,
 And ſtalde the deare that thou ſhouldſt ſtrike,
Let reaſon rule things worthy blame,
As well as fancy(partyall might)
 Take counſell of ſome wiſer head,
 Neither too young, nor yet vnwed.

And when thon comſt thy tale to tell,
Smooth not thy toung with filed talke,
Leaſt ſhe ſome ſubtill practiſe ſmell,
A Cripple ſoone can finde a halt,
 But plainly ſay thou louſt her well,
 And ſet her perſon forth to ſale.

                    D

What though her frowning browes be bent
Her cloudy lookes will calme yer night,
And then too late she will repent,
That thus dissembled her delight.
  And twice desire yer it be day,
  That which with scorne she put away.

What though she striue to try her strength,
And ban and braule, and say the nay:
Her feeble force will yeeld at length,
When craft hath taught her thus to say:
  Had women beene so strong as men
  In faith you had not had it then.

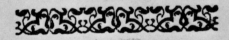

And to her will frame all thy waies,
Spare not to spend, and chiefly there,
Where thy desart may merit praise,
By ringiug in thy Ladies eare,
   The strongest castle, tower and towne,
   The golden bullet beats it downe.

Serue alwaies with assured trust,
And in thy sute be humble true,
Vnlesse thy Lady proue vniust,
Prease neuer thou to chuse a new:
   When time shall serue, be thou not slacke,
   To proffer thongh she put thee back.

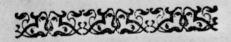

The wiles and guiles that women worke,
Dissembled with an outward shew:
The tricks and toyes that in them lurke,
The Cock that treads thē shall not know,
   Haue you not heard it said full oft,
   A Womans nay doth stand for nought.

Thinke Women still to striue with men,
To sinne and neuer for to faint,
There is no heauen(by holy then)
When time with age shall them attaine,
   Were kisses all the ioyes in bed,
   One Woman would another wed.

But soft enough,too much I feare,
Least that my mistresse heare my song,
She will not stick to round me on th'are,
To teach my toung to be so long:
   Yet will she blush,here be it said,
   To heare her secrets so bewraid.

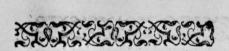

XIX

L Iue with me and be my Loue,
  And we will all the pleasures proue .
That hilles and vallies, dales and fields,
And all the craggy mountaines yeeld.

There will we sit vpon the Rocks,
And see the Shepheards feed their flocks,
By shallow Riuers, by whose fals
Melodious birds sing Madrigals.

There will I make thee a bed of Roses,
With a thousand fragrant poses,
A cap of flowers, and a Kirtle
Imbrodered all with leaues of Mirtle.

A belt of ftraw and Yuye buds,
With Corall Clafps and Amber ftuds,
And if thefe pleafures may thee moue,
Then liue with me, and be my Loue.

Loues anfwere.

IF that the World and Loue were young,
And truth in euery fhepheards toung,
Thefe pretty pleafures might me moue,
To liue with thee and be thy Loue.

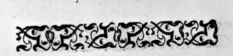

XX

AS it fell vpon a Day,
 In the merry Month of May,
Sitting in a pleasant shade,
Which a groue of Myrtles made,
Beastes did leape, and Birds did sing,
Trees did grow, and Plants did spring:
Euery thing did banish mone,
Saue the Nightingale alone,
Shee(poore Bird)as all forlorne,
Leand her breast vp-till a thorne,
And there sung the dolefulst Ditty,
That to heare it was great Pitty,
Fie, fie, fie, now would she cry
Teru, Teru, by and by:

That to heare her so complaine,
Scarce I could from teares refraine:
For her griefes so liuely showne,
Made me thinke vpon mine owne.
Ah(thought I)thou mournst in vaine,
None takes pitty on thy paine:
Senslesse Trees, they cannot heare thee,
Ruthlesse Beares, they will not cheere thee.
King Pandion, he is dead:
All thy friends are lapt in Lead.
All thy fellow Birds doe sing,
Carelesse of thy sorrowing.

Whilſt as fickle Fortune ſmilde,
Thou and I, were both beguild.
Euery one that flatters thee,
Is no friend in miſerie:
Words are eaſie, like the wind,
Faithfull friends are hard to find:
Euery man will be thy friend,
Whilſt thou haſt wherewith to ſpend:
But if ſtore of Crownes be ſcant,
No man will ſupply thy want
If that one be prodigall,
Bountifull they will him call:
And with ſuch-like flattering,
Pitty but he were a King.

If he be addict to vice,
Quickly him, they will intice.
If to Women hee be bent,
They haue at Commaundement.
But if Fortune once doe frowne,
Then farewell his great renowne:
They that fawnd on him before,
Vse his company no more.
Hee that is thy friend indeede,
Hee will helpe thee in thy neede:
If thou sorrow, he will weepe :
If thou wake, hee cannot sleepe:
Thus of euery griefe, in hart
Hee, with thee, doeth beare a part.
These are certaine signes, to know
Faithfull friend, from flatt'ring foe.

THE PASSIONATE PILGRIM

FRAGMENTS OF THE FIRST EDITION

1599 ?

The Folger Library Copy

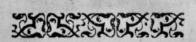

WHen my Loue sweares that she is made of truth,
I do beleeue her (though I know she lies)
That she might thinke me some vntutor'd youth,
Vnskilful in the worlds false forgeries.
Thus vainly thinking that she thinkes me young,
Although I know my yeares be past the best:
I smiling, credite her false speaking toung,
Outfacing faults in loue, with loues ill rest.
But wherefore sayes my loue that she is young?
And wherefore say not I, that I am old:
O, Loues best habit's in a soothing toung,
And Age in loue, loues not to haue yeares told.
　　Therefore I'le lye with Loue, and loue with me,
　　Since that our faultes in loue thus smother'd be.

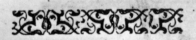

TWo loues I haue, of Comfort and Despaire,
　That like two Spirits, do suggest me still:
My better Angell, is a Man (right faire)
My worser spirite a Woman (colour'd ill.)
To win me soone to hell, my Female euill
Tempteth my better Angell from my side:
And would corrupt my Saint to be a Diuell,
Wooing his puritie with her faire pride.
And whether that my Angell be turnde feend,
Suspect I may (yet not directly tell:)
For being both to me; both, to each friend,
I ghesse one Angell in anothers hell:
　The truth I shall not know, but liue in dout,
　Till my bad Angell fire my good one out.

DYd not the heauenly Rhetoricke of thine eie,
  Gainſt whom the world could not hold argumen
Perſwade my hart to this falſe periury;
Vowes for thee broke deſerue not puniſhment.
A woman I forſwore : but I will proue
Thou being a goddeſſe, I forſwore not thee:
My vow was earthly, thou a heauenly loue,
Thy grace being gainde, cures al diſgrace in me.
My vow was breath, and breath a vapor is,
  Then thou faire Sun, that on this earth doth ſhine,
Exhalt this vapor vow, in thee it is:
If broken, then it is no fault of mine.
    If by me broke, what foole is not ſo wiſe
    To breake an oth, to win a paradiſe?

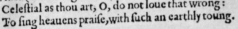

IF loue make me forſworne, how ſhal I ſwere to loue?
  O, neuer faith could hold, if not to beauty vowed:
Though to my ſelfe forſworne, to thee Ile conſtāt proue,
thoſe thoghts to me like Okes, to thee like Oſiers bowed.
Studdy his byas leaues, & makes his booke thine eies,
Where al thoſe pleaſures liue, that Art can cōprehend:
If knowledge be the marke, to know thee ſhal ſuffice:
Wel learned is that toung that wel can thee commend.
All ignorant that ſoule, that ſees thee without wonder,
Which is to me ſome praiſe, that I thy parts admyre :
Thin eye Ioues lightning ſeems, thy voice his dredful thū
Which (not to anger bent) is muſick & ſweet fire. (der,
  Celeſtial as thou art, O, do not loue that wrong :
  To ſing heauens praiſe, with ſuch an earthly toung.

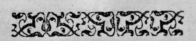

ON a day (alack the day,)
  Loue whofe month was ener May:
Spied a bloffome paffing faire,
Playing in the wanton ayre,
Through the veluet leaues the winde
All vnfeen gan paffage find,
That the louer (ficke to death,)
Wifht himfelfe the heauens breath,
Ayre (quoth he) thy cheeks may blowe,
Ayre, would I might triumph fo
But (alas) my hand hath fworne,
Nere to pruck thee from thy throne,
Vow (allcke) for youth vnmeet,
Youth, fo apt to pluck a fweet,
Thou for whom Ioue would fweare,
Iuno but an Ethiope were
And deny himfelfe for Ioue,
Turning mortal for thy Lous.

Shakespeare's Poem on the Subject:

THE PHOENIX AND TURTLE

from

LOVE'S MARTYR

FIRST EDITION

1601

The Folger Library Copy

LOVES MARTYR:
OR,
ROSALINS COMPLAINT.

Allegorically shadowing the truth of Loue,
in the conftant Fate of the Phœnix
and Turtle.

A Poeme enterlaced with much varietie and raritie;
now firft tranflated out of the venerable Italian Torquato
Cæliano, *by* ROBERT CHESTER.

With the true legend of famous King *Arthur*, the laft of the nine
Worthies, being the firft *Effay* of a new *Brytifh* Poet: collected
out of diuerfe Authenticall Records.

To thefe are added fome new compofitions, of feuerall moderne Writers
whofe names are fubfcribed to their feuerall workes, vpon the
firft Subiect : viz. the Phœnix *and*
Turtle.

Mar: —————— *Mutare dominum non poteft liber notus.*

LONDON
Imprinted for E. B.
1601.

HEREAFTER
FOLLOVV DIVERSE
Poeticall Essaies on the former Subiect; viz: the *Turtle* and *Phœnix*.

Done by the best and chiefest of our
moderne writers, with their names subscribed to their particular workes:
neuer before extant.

And (now first) consecrated by them all generally,
to the loue and merite of the true-noble Knight,
Sir Iohn Salisburie.

Dignum laude virum Musa vetat mori.

MDCI.

Let the bird of lowdeſt lay,
On the ſole *Arabian* tree,
Herauld ſad and trumpet be:
To whoſe ſound chaſte wings obay.

But thou ſhriking harbinger,
Foule precurrer of the fiend,
Augour of the feuers end,
To this troupe come thou not neere.

From this Seſſion interdict
Euery ſoule of tyrant wing,
Saue the Eagle feath'red King,
Keepe the obſequie ſo ſtrict.

Let the Prieſt in Surples white,
That defunctiue Muſicke can,
Be the death-deui ning Swan,
Leſt the *Requiem* lacke his right.

And thou treble dated Crow,
That thy ſable gender mak'ſt,
With the breath thou giu'ſt and tak'ſt,
Mongſt our mourners ſhalt thou go.

Here the Antheme doth commence,
Loue and Conſtancie is dead,
Phœnix and the *Turtle* fled,
In a mutuall flame from hence.

So they loued as loue in twaine,
Had the eſſence but in one,

Two

234

Two diſtincts, Diuiſion none,
Number there in loue was ſlaine.

Hearts remote, yet not aſunder;
Diſtance and no ſpace was ſeene,
Twixt this *Turtle* and his Queene;
But in them it were a wonder.

So betweene them Loue did ſhine,
That the *Turtle* ſaw his right,
Flaming in the *Phœnix* ſight;
Either was the others mine.

Propertie was thus appalled,
That the ſelfe was not the ſame:
Single Natures double name,
Neither two nor one was called.

Reaſon in it ſelfe confounded,
Saw Diuiſion grow together,
To themſelues yet either neither,
Simple were ſo well compounded.

That it cried, how true a twaine,
Seemeth this concordant one,
Loue hath Reaſon, Reaſon none,
If what parts, can ſo remaine.

Whereupon it made this *Threne*,
To the *Phœnix* and the *Doue*,
Co-ſupremes and ſtarres of Loue,
As *Chorus* to their Tragique Scene.

Threnos.

BEautie, Truth, and Raritie,
Grace in all ſimplicitie,
Here encloſde, in cinders lie.

Death is now the *Phœnix* neſt,
And the *Turtles* loyall breſt,
To eternitie doth reſt.

Leauing no poſteritie,
Twas not their infirmitie,
It was married Chaſtitie.

Truth may ſeeme, but cannot be,
Beautie bragge, but tis not ſhe,
Truth and Beautie buried be.

To this vrne let thoſe repaire,
That are either true or faire,
For theſe dead Birds, ſigh a prayer.

William Shake-ſpeare.

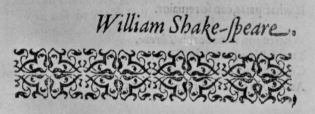

SHAKESPEARE'S SONNETS

and

A LOVER'S COMPLAINT

FIRST EDITION

1609

The Elizabethan Club Copy

SHAKE-SPEARES

SONNETS.

Neuer before Imprinted.

AT LONDON
By *G. Eld* for *T. T.* and are
to be folde by *Iohn Wright,* dwelling
at Chrift Church gate.
1609.

TO.THE.ONLIE.BEGETTER.OF.
THESE.INSVING.SONNETS.
M^r.W.H. ALL.HAPPINESSE.
AND.THAT.ETERNITIE.
PROMISED.

BY.

OVR.EVER-LIVING.POET.

WISHETH.

THE.WELL-WISHING.
ADVENTVRER.IN.
SETTING.
(FORTH.

T.T.

Shake-speares,
SONNETS.

FRom faireſt creatures we deſire increaſe,
    That thereby beauties *Roſe* might neuer die,
But as the riper ſhould by time deceaſe,
His tender heire might beare his memory:
But thou contracted to thine owne bright eyes,
Feed'ſt thy lights flame with ſelfe ſubſtantiall fewell,
Making a famine where aboundance lies,
Thy ſelfe thy foe, to thy ſweet ſelfe too cruell:
Thou that art now the worlds freſh ornament,
And only herauld to the gaudy ſpring,
Within thine owne bud burieſt thy content,
And tender chorle makſt waſt in niggarding:
    Pitty the world, or elſe this glutton be,
    To eate the worlds due, by the graue and thee.

2

VVHen fortie Winters ſhall beſeige thy brow,
    And digge deep trenches in thy beauties field,
Thy youthes proud liuery ſo gaz'd on now,
Wil be a totter'd weed of ſmal worth held:
Then being askt, where all thy beautie lies,
Where all the treaſure of thy luſty daies;
To ſay within thine owne deepe ſunken eyes,
Were an all-eating ſhame, and thriftleſſe praiſe.
How much more praiſe deſeru'd thy beauties vſe,
If thou couldſt anſwere this faire child of mine
Shall ſum my count, and make my old excuſe
Proouing his beautie by ſucceſſion thine.

B

This

This were to be new made when thou art ould,
And see thy blood warme when thou feel'st it could,

3

Looke in thy glaffe and tell the face thou vewest,
Now is the time that face fhould forme an other,
Whofe frefh repaire if now thou not reneweft,
Thou doo'ft beguile the world, vnbleffe fome mother.
For where is fhe fo faire whofe vn-eard wombe
Difdaines the tillage of thy husbandry?
Or who is he fo fond will be the tombe,
Of his felfe loue to ftop pofterity?
Thou art thy mothers glaffe and fhe in thee
Calls backe the louely Aprill of her prime,
So thou through windowes of thine age fhalt fee,
Difpight of wrinkles this thy goulden time.
　　But if thou liue remembred not to be,
　　Die fingle and thine Image dies with thee.

4

VNthrifty louelineffe why doft thou spend,
Vpon thy felfe thy beauties legacy?
Natures bequeft giues nothing but doth lend,
And being franck fhe lends to thofe are free:
Then beautious nigard why dooft thou abufe,
The bountious largeffe giuen thee to giue?
Profitles vferer why dooft thou vfe
So great a fumme of fummes yet can'ft not liue?
For hauing traffike with thy felfe alone,
Thou of thy felfe thy fweet felfe doft deceaue,
Then how when nature calls thee to be gone,
What acceptable *Audit* can'ft thou leaue?
　　Thy vnuf'd beauty muft be tomb'd with thee,
　　Which vfed liues th'executor to be.

5

THofe howers that with gentle worke did frame,
The louely gaze where euery eye doth dwell
Will play the tirants to the very fame,

　　　　　　　　　　　　　　　　And

And that vnfaire which fairely doth excell:
For neuer resting time leads Summer on,
To hidious winter and confounds him there,
Sap checkt with frost and lustie leau's quite gon,
Beauty ore-snow'd and barenes euery where,
Then were not summers distillation left
A liquid prisoner pent in walls of glasse,
Beauties effect with beauty were bereft,
Nor it nor noe remembrance what it was.
   But flowers distil'd though they with winter meete,
   Leese but their show,their substance still liues sweet.

6

THen let not winters wragged hand deface,
  In thee thy summer ere thou be distil'd:
Make sweet some viall;treasure thou some place,
With beautits treasure ere it be selfe kil'd:
That vse is not forbidden vsery,
Which happies those that pay the willing lone;
That's for thy selfe to breed an other thee,
Or ten times happier be it ten for one,
Ten times thy selfe were happier then thou art,
If ten of thine ten times refigur'd thee,
Then what could death doe if thou should'st depart,
Leauing thee liuing in posterity?
   Be not selfe-wild for thou art much too faire,
   To be deaths conquest and make wormes thine heire.

7

LOe in the Orient when the gracious light,
  Lifts vp his burning head,each vnder eye
Doth homage to his new appearing sight,
Seruing with lookes his sacred maiesty,
And hauing climb'd the steepe vp heauenly hill,
Resembling strong youth in his middle age,
Yet mortall lookes adore his beauty still,
Attending on his goulden pilgrimage:
But when from high-most pich with wery car,

B 2

Like

Like feeble age he reeleth from the day,
The eyes(fore dutious)now conuerted are
From his low tract and looke an other way:
  So thou,thy selfe out-going in thy noon:
  Vnlok'd on dieft vnleffe thou get a fonne.

8

MVfick to heare,why hear'ft thou mufick fadly,
Sweets with fweets warre not , ioy delights in ioy:
Why lou'ft thou that which thou receauft not gladly,
Or elfe receau'ft with pleafure thine annoy ?
If the true concord of well tuned founds,
By vnions married do offend thine eare,
They do but fweetly chide thee, who confounds
In fingleneffe the parts that thou fhould'ft beare:
Marke how one ftring fweet husband to an other,
Strikes each in each by mutuall ordering;
Refembling fier,and child, and happy mother,
Who all in one,one pleafing note do fing:
  Whofe fpeechleffe fong being many,feeming one,
  Sings this to thee thou fingle wilt proue none.

9.

IS it for feare to wet a widdowes eye,
That thou confum'ft thy felfe in fingle life?
Ah;if thou iffuleffe fhalt hap to die,
The world will waile thee like a makeleffe wife,
The world wilbe thy widdow and ftill weepe,
That thou no forme of thee haft left behind,
When euery priuat widdow well may keepe,
By childrens eyes,her husbands fhape in minde:
Looke what an vnthrift in the world doth spend
Shifts but his place,for ftill the world inioyes it
But beauties wafte hath in the world an end,
And kept vnvfde the vfer fo deftroyes it:
  No loue toward others in that bofome fits
  That on himfelfe fuch murdrous fhame commits.

10

FOr ſhame deny that thou bear'ſt loue to any
Who for thy ſelfe art ſo vnprouident
Graunt if thou wilt,thou art belou'd of many,
But that thou none lou'ſt is moſt euident:
For thou art ſo poſſeſt with murdrous hate,
That gainſt thy ſelfe thou ſtickſt not to conſpire,
Seeking that beautious rooſe to ruinate
Which to repaire ſhould be thy chiefe deſire :
O change thy thought,that I may change my minde,
Shall hate be fairer log'd then gentle loue?
Be as thy preſence is gracious and kind,
Or to thy ſelfe at leaſt kind harted proue,
   Make thee an other ſelfe for loue of me,
   That beauty ſtill may liue in thine or thee.

11

AS faſt as thou ſhalt wane ſo faſt thou grow'ſt,
In one of thine,from that which thou departeſt,
And that freſh bloud which yongly thou beſtow'ſt,
Thou maiſt call thine,when thou from youth conuerteſt,
Herein liues wiſdome,beauty,and increaſe,
Without this follie,age,and could decay,
If all were minded ſo,the times ſhould ceaſe,
And threeſcoore yeare would make the world away:
Let thoſe whom nature hath not made for ſtore,
Harſh,featureleſſe,and rude , barrenly perriſh,
Looke whom ſhe beſt indow'd,ſhe gaue the more;
Which bountious guiſt thou ſhouldſt in bounty cherriſh,
   She caru'd thee for her ſeale,and ment therby,
   Thou ſhouldſt print more,not let that coppy die.

12

VVHen I doe count the clock that tels the time,
   And ſee the braue day ſunck in hidious night,
When I behold the violet paſt prime,
And ſable curls or ſiluer'd ore with white :
When lofty trees I ſee barren of leaues,
Which erſt from heat did canopie the herd

B3

And

And Sommers greene all girded vp in sheaues
Borne on the beare with white and bristly beard:
Then of thy beauty do I question make
That thou among the wastes of time must goe,
Since sweets and beauties do them-selues forsake,
    And die as fast as they see others grow,
        And nothing gainst Times sieth can make defence
        Saue breed to braue him, when he takes thee hence.

13

O That you were your selfe, but loue you are
    No longer yours, then you your selfe here liue,
Against this cumming end you should prepare,
And your sweet semblance to some other giue.
So should that beauty which you hold in lease
Find no determination, then you were
You selfe again after your selfes decease,
When your sweet issue your sweet forme should beare.
Who lets so faire a house fall to decay,
Which husbandry in honour might vphold,
Against the stormy gusts of winters day
And barren rage of deaths eternall cold?
    O none but vnthrifts, deare my loue you know,
    You had a Father, let your Son say so.

14

NOt from the stars do I my iudgement plucke,
    And yet me thinkes I haue Astronomy,
But not to tell of good, or euil lucke,
Of plagues, of dearths, or seasons quallity,
Nor can I fortune to breefe mynuits tell;
Pointing to each his thunder, raine and winde,
Or say with Princes if it shal go wel
By oft predict that I in heauen finde.
But from thine eies my knowledge I deriue,
And constant stars in them I read such art
As truth and beautie shal together thriue
If from thy selfe, to store thou wouldst conuert:

Of

Or elfe of thee this I prognofticate,
Thy end is Truthes and Beauties doome and date.

15

WHen I confider euery thing that growes
Holds in perfection but a little moment.
That this huge ftage prefenteth nought but fhowes
Whereon the Stars in fecret influence comment.
When I perceiue that men as plants increafe,
Cheared and checkt euen by the felfe-fame skie:
Vaunt in their youthfull fap, at height decreafe,
And were their braue ftate out of memory.
Then the conceit of this inconftant ftay,
Sets you moft rich in youth before my fight,
Where waftfull time debateth with decay
To change your day of youth to fullied night,
   And all in war with Time for loue of you
   As he takes from you, I ingraft you new.

16

BVt wherefore do not you a mightier waie
Make warre vppon this bloudie tirant time?
And fortifie your felfe in your decay
With meanes more bleffed then my barren rime?
Now ftand you on the top of happie houres,
And many maiden gardens yet vnfet,
With vertuous wifh would beare your liuing flowers,
Much liker then your painted counterfeit:
So fhould the lines of life that life repaire
Which this (Times penfel or my pupill pen)
Neither in inward worth nor outward faire
Can make you liue your felfe in eies of men,
   To giue away your felfe, keeps your felfe ftill,
   And you muft liue drawne by your owne fweet skill,

17

VVHo will beleeue my verfe in time to come
If it were fild with your moft high deferts?
     Though

Though yet heauen knowes it is but as a tombe
Which hides your life , and fhewes not halfe your parts:
If I could write the beauty of your eyes,
And in frefh numbers number all your graces,
The age to come would fay this Poet lies,
Such heauenly touches nere toucht earthly faces.
So fhould my papers (yellowed with their age)
Be fcorn'd,like old men of leffe truth then tongue,
And your true rights be termd a Poets rage,
And ftretched miter of an Antique fong.
　　But were fome childe of yours aliue that time,
　　You fhould liue twife in it,and in my rime.

18.

SHall I compare thee to a Summers day?
Thou art more louely and more temperate:
Rough windes do fhake the darling buds of Maie,
And Sommers leafe hath all too fhort a date:
Sometime too hot the eye of heauen fhines,
And often is his gold complexion dimm'd,
And euery faire from faire fome-time declines,
By chance,or natures changing courfe vntrim'd:
But thy eternall Sommer fhall not fade,
Nor loofe poffeffion of that faire thou ow'ft,
Nor fhall death brag thou wandr'ft in his fhade,
When in eternall lines to time thou grow'ft,
　　So long as men can breath or eyes can fee,
　　So long liues this,and this giues life to thee,

19

DEuouring time blunt thou the Lyons pawes,
And make the earth deuoure her owne fweet brood,
Plucke the keene teeth from the fierce Tygers yawes,
And burne the long liu'd Phænix in her blood,
Make glad and forry feafons as thou fleet'ft,
And do what ere thou wilt fwift-footed time
To the wide world and all her fading fweets:
But I forbid thee one moft hainous crime,

O

O carue not with thy howers my loues faire brow,
Nor draw noe lines there with thine antique pen,
Him in thy course vntainted doe allow,
For beauties patterne to succeding men.
    Yet doe thy worst ould Time dispight thy wrong,
    My loue shall in my verse euer liue young.

20

A Womans face with natures owne hand painted,
  Haste thou the Master Mistris of my passion,
A womans gentle hart but not acquainted
With shifting change as is false womens fashion,
An eye more bright then theirs, lesse false in rowling:
Gilding the obiect where-vpon it gazeth,
A man in hew all *Hews* in his controwling,
Which steales mens eyes and womens soules amaseth.
And for a woman wert thou first created,
Till nature as she wrought thee fell a dotinge,
And by addition me of thee defeated,
By adding one thing to my purpose nothing.
    But since she prickt thee out for womens pleasure,
    Mine be thy loue and thy loues vse their treasure.

21

SO is it not with me as with that Muse,
  Stird by a painted beauty to his verse,
Who heauen it selfe for ornament doth vse,
And euery faire with his faire doth reherse,
Making a coopelment of proud compare
With Sunne and Moone, with earth and seas rich gems:
With Aprills first borne flowers and all things rare,
That heauens ayre in this huge rondure hems,
O let me true in loue but truly write,
And then beleeue me, my loue is as faire,
As any mothers childe, though not so bright
As those gould candells fixt in heauens ayer:
    Let them say more that like of heare-say well,
    I will not prayse that purpose not to sell.

C   22

22

MY glaſſe ſhall not perſwade me I am ould,
So long as youth and thou are of one date,
But when in thee times forrwes I behould,
Then look I death my daies ſhould expiate.
For all that beauty that doth couer thee,
Is but the ſeemly rayment of my heart,
Which in thy breſt doth liue, as thine in me,
How can I then be elder then thou art?
O therefore loue be of thy ſelfe ſo wary,
As I not for my ſelfe, but for thee will,
Bearing thy heart which I will keepe ſo chary
As tender nurſe her babe from faring ill,
 Preſume not on thy heart when mine is ſlaine,
 Thou gau'ſt me thine not to giue backe againe.

23

AS an vnperfect actor on the ſtage,
Who with his feare is put beſides his part,
Or ſome fierce thing repleat with too much rage,
Whoſe ſtrengths abondance weakens his owne heart;
So I for feare of truſt, forget to ſay,
The perfect ceremony of loues right,
And in mine owne loues ſtrength ſeeme to decay,
Ore-charg'd with burthen of mine owne loues might:
O let my books be then the eloquence,
And domb preſagers of my ſpeaking breſt,
Who pleade for loue, and look for recompence,
More then that tonge that more hath more expreſt.
 O learne to read what ſilent loue hath writ,
 To heare wit eies belongs to loues fine wiht.

24

MIne eye hath play'd the painter and hath ſteeld,
Thy beauties forme in table of my heart,
My body is the frame wherein ti's held,
And perſpectiue it is beſt Painters art.
For through the Painter muſt you ſee his skill,

         To

To finde where your true Image pictur'd lies,
Which in my bosomes shop is hanging stil,
That hath his windowes glazed with thine eyes:
Now see what good-turnes eyes for eies haue done,
Mine eyes haue drawne thy shape,and thine for me
Are windowes to my brest, where-through the Sun
Delights to peepe,to gaze therein on thee
  Yet eyes this cunning want to grace their art
  They draw but what they see,know not the hart.

25

LEt those who are in fauor with their stars,
Of publike honour and proud titles bost,
Whilst I whome fortune of such tryumph bars
Vnlookt for ioy in that I honour most;
Great Princes fauorites their faire leaues spread,
But as the Marygold at the suns eye,
And in them-selues their pride lies buried,
For at a frowne they in their glory die.
The painefull warrier famosed for worth,
After a thousand victories once foild,
Is from the booke of honour rased quite,
And all the rest forgot for which he toild:
  Then happy I that loue and am beloued
  Where I may not remoue,nor be remoued.

26

LOrd of my loue,to whome in vassalage
Thy merrit hath my dutie strongly knit;
To thee I send this written ambassage
To witnesse duty, not to shew my wit.
Duty so great,which wit so poore as mine
May make seeme bare,in wanting words to shew it;
But that I hope some good conceipt of thine
In thy soules thought(all naked) will bestow it:
Til whatsoeuer star that guides my mouing,
Points on me gratiously with faire aspect,
And puts apparrell on my tottered louing,

C 2   To

To show me worthy of their sweet respect,
Then may I dare to boast how I doe loue thee,
Til then,not show my head where thou maist proue me.

27

WEary with toyle,I hast me to my bed,
  The deare repose for lims with trauaill tired,
But then begins a iourny in my head
To worke my mind,when boddies work's expired.
For then my thoughts(from far where I abide)
Intend a zelous pilgrimage to thee,
And keepe my drooping eye-lids open wide,
Looking on darknes which the blind doe see.
Saue that my soules imaginary sight
Presents their shaddoe to my sightles view,
Which like a iewell(hunge in gastly night)
Makes blacke night beautious,and her old face new,
  Loe thus by day my lims,by night my mind,
  For thee,and for my selfe,noe quiet finde.

28

HOw can I then returne in happy plight
  That am debard the benifit of rest?
When daies oppression is not eazd by night,
But day by night and night by day oprest.
And each(though enimes to ethers raigne)
Doe in consent shake hands to torture me,
The one by toyle,the other to complaine
How far I toyle,still farther off from thee.
I tell the Day to please him thou art bright,
And do'st him grace when clouds doe blot the heauen:
So flatter I the swart complexiond night,
When sparkling stars twire not thou guil'st th'eauen.
  But day doth daily draw my sorrowes longer,(stronger
  And night doth nightly make greefes length seeme

29

VVHen in disgrace with Fortune and mens eyes,
  I all alone beweepe my out-cast state,

And

And trouble deafe heauen with my bootleſſe cries,
And looke vpon my ſelfe and curſe my fate.
Wiſhing me like to one more rich in hope,
Featur'd like him,like him with friends poſſeſt,
Deſiring this mans art,and that mans skope,
With what I moſt inioy contented leaſt,
Yet in theſe thoughts my ſelfe almoſt deſpiſing,
Haplye I thinke on thee, and then my ſtate,
(Like to the Larke at breake of daye ariſing)
From ſullen earth ſings himns at Heauens gate,
  For thy ſweet loue remembred ſuch welth brings,
  That then I skorne to change my ſtate with Kings.

30

VVHen to the Seſſions of ſweet ſilent thought,
  I ſommon vp remembrance of things paſt,
I ſigh the lacke of many a thing I ſought,
And with old woes new waile my deare times waſte:
Then can I drowne an eye(vn-vſ'd to flow)
For precious friends hid in deaths dateles night,
And weepe a freſh loues long ſince canceld woe,
And mone th'expence of many a vanniſht ſight.
Then can I greeue at greeuances fore-gon,
And heauily from woe to woe tell ore
The ſad account of fore-bemoned mone,
Which I new pay as if not payd before:
  But if the while I thinke on thee (deare friend)
  All loſſes are reſtord,and ſorrowes end.

31

Thy boſome is indeared with all hearts,
  Which I by lacking haue ſuppoſed dead,
And there raignes Loue and all Loues louing parts,
And all thoſe friends which I thought buried.
How many a holy and obſequious teare
Hath deare religious loue ſtolne from mine eye,
As intereſt of the dead,which now appeare,
But things remou'd that hidden in there lie.

Thou art the graue where buried loue doth liue,
Hung with the tropheis of my louers gon,
Who all their parts of me to thee did giue,
That due of many, now is thine alone.
   Their images I lou'd, I view in thee,
   And thou(all they)haft all the all of me.

32

IF thou furuiue my well contented daie,
  When that churle death my bones with duft shall couer
And shalt by fortune once more re-furuay:
These poore rude lines of thy deceafed Louer:
Compare them with the bett'ring of the time,
And though they be out-ftript by euery pen,
Referue them for my loue, not for their rime,
Exceeded by the hight of happier men.
Oh then voutfafe me but this louing thought,
Had my friends Muse growne with this growing age,
A dearer birth then this his loue had brought
To march in ranckes of better equipage:
   But fince he died and Poets better proue,
   Theirs for their ftile ile read, his for his loue.

33

FVll many a glorious morning haue I feene,
  Flatter the mountaine tops with foueraine eie,
Kiffing with golden face the meddowes greene;
Guilding pale ftreames with heauenly alcumy:
Anon permit the bafeft cloudes to ride,
With ougly rack on his celeftiall face,
And from the fol-lorne world his vifage hide
Stealing vn'eene to weft with this difgrace:
Euen fo my Sunne one early morne did shine,
With all triumphant fplendor on my brow,
But out alack, he was but one houre mine,
The region cloude hath mask'd him from me now.
   Yet him for this, my loue no whit difdaineth,
   Suns of the world may ftaine, whē heauens fun ftainteh.

34

34

VVHy didſt thou promiſe ſuch a beautious day,
　　And make me trauaile forth without my cloake,
To let baſe cloudes ore-take me in my way,
Hiding thy brau'ry in their rotten ſmoke.
Tis not enou h that through the cloude thou breake,
To dry the raine on my ſtorme-beaten face,
For no man well of ſuch aſalue can ſpeake,
That heales the wound, and cures not the diſgrace:
Nor can thy ſhame giue phiſicke to my griefe,
Though thou repent , yet I haue ſtill the loſſe,
Th'offenders ſorrow lends but weake reliefe
To him that beares the ſtrong offenſes loſſe.
　　Ah but thoſe teares are pearle which thy loue ſheeds,
　　And they are ritch, and ranſome all ill deeds.

35

NO more bee greeu'd at that which thou haſt done,
　　Roſes haue thornes; and ſiluer fountaines mud,
Cloudes and eclipſes ſtaine both Moone and Sunne,
And loathſome canker liues in ſweeteſt bud.
All men make faults, and euen I in this,
Authorizing thy treſpas with compare,
My ſelfe corrupting ſaluing thy amiſſe,
Excuſing their ſins more then their ſins are:
For to thy ſenſuall fault I bring in ſence,
Thy aduerſe party is thy Aduocate,
And gainſt my ſelfe a lawfull plea commence,
Such ciuill war is in my loue and hate,
　　That I an acceſſary needs muſt be,
　　To that ſweet theefe which ſourely robs from me,

36

LEt me confeſſe that we two muſt be twaine,
　　Although our vndeuided loues are one:
So ſhall thoſe blots that do with me remaine,
Without thy helpe, by me be borne alone.
In our two loues there is but one reſpect,

Though

Though in our liues a feperable fpight,
Which though it alter not loues fole effect,
Yet doth it fteale fweet houres from loues delight,
I may not euer-more acknowledge thee,
Leaft my bewailed guilt fhould do thee fhame,
Nor thou with publike kindneffe honour me,
Vnleffe thou take that honour from thy name:
    But doe not fo,I loue thee in fuch fort,
    As thou being mine,mine is thy good report.

37

A S a decrepit father takes delight,
  To fee his actiue childe do deeds of youth,
So I, made lame by Fortunes deareft fpight
Take all my comfort of thy worth and truth.
For whether beauty,birth,or wealth,or wit,
Or any of thefe all,or all,or more
Intitled in their parts,do crowned fit,
I make my loue ingrafted to this ftore:
So then I am not lame,poore, nor difpif'd,
Whilft that this fhadow doth fuch fubftance giue,
That I in thy abundance am fuffic'd,
And by a part of all thy glory liue:
    Looke what is beft,that beft I wifh in thee,
    This wifh I haue,then ten times happy me.

38

H Ow can my Mufe want fubiect to inuent
  While thou doft breath that poor'ft into my verfe,
Thine owne fweet argument,to excellent,
For euery vulgar paper to rehearfe:
Oh giue thy felfe the thankes if ought in me,
Worthy perufal ftand againft thy fight,
For who's fo dumbe that cannot write to thee,
When thou thy felfe doft giue inuention light?
Be thou the tenth Mufe,ten times more in worth
Then thofe old nine which rimers inuocate,
And he that calls on thee,let him bring forth

Eternall

Eternal numbers to out-liue long date.
  If my slight Muse doe pleafe thefe curious daies,
  The paine be mine,but thine fhal be the praife.

39

OH how thy worth with manners may I finge,
  When thou art all the better part of me?
What can mine owne praife to mine owne felfe bring;
And what is't but mine owne when I praife thee,
Euen for this,let vs deuided liue,
And our deare loue loofe name of fingle one,
That by this feperation I may giue:
That due to thee which thou deferu'ft alone:
Oh abfence what a torment wouldft thou proue,
Were it not thy foure leifure gaue fweet leaue,
To entertaine the time with thoughts of loue,
VVhich time and thoughts fo fweetly doft deceiue.
  And that thou teacheft how to make one twaine,
  By praifing him here who doth hence remaine.

40

TAke all my loues,my loue,yea take them all,
  What haft thou then more then thou hadft before?
No loue,my loue,that thou maift true loue call,
All mine was thine,before thou hadft this more:
Then if for my loue,thou my loue receiueft,
I cannot blame thee,for my loue thou vfeft,
But yet be blam'd,if thou this felfe deceaueft
By wilfull tafte of what thy felfe refufeft.
I doe forgiue thy robb'rie gentle theefe
Although thou fteale thee all my pouerty:
And yet loue knowes it is a greater griefe
To beare loues wrong,then hates knowne iniury.
  Lafciuious grace,in whom all il wel fhowes,
  Kill me with fpights yet we muft not be foes.

41

THofe pretty wrongs that liberty commits,
  When I am some-time abfent from thy heart,

D   Thy

Thy beautie,and thy yeares full well befits,
For still temptation followes where thou art.
Gentle thou art,and therefore to be wonne,
Beautious thou art,therefore to be affailed.
And when a woman woes,what womans fonne,
Will fourely leaue her till he haue preuailed.
Aye me,but yet thou mighft my feate forbeare,
And chide thy beauty,and thy ftraying youth,
Who lead thee in their ryot euen there
Where thou art forft to breake a two-fold truth:
 Hers by thy beauty tempting her to thee,
 Thine by thy beautie beeing false to me.

42

THat thou haft her it is not all my griefe,
 And yet it may be faid I lou'd her deerely,
That fhe hath thee is of my wayling cheefe,
A loffe in loue that touches me more neerely.
Louing offendors thus I will excufe yee,
Thou dooft loue her,becaufe thou knowft I loue her,
And for my fake euen fo doth fhe abufe me,
Suffring my friend for my fake to approoue her,
If I loofe thee,my loffe is my loues gaine,
And loofing her,my friend hath found that loffe,
Both finde each other,and I loofe both twaine,
And both for my fake lay on me this croffe,
 But here's the ioy,my friend and I are one,
 Sweete flattery,then fhe loues but me alone.

43

WHen moft I winke then doe mine eyes beft fee,
 For all the day they view things vnrefpected,
But when I fleepe,in dreames they looke on thee,
And darkely bright,are bright in darke directed.
Then thou whofe fhaddow fhaddowes doth make bright,
How would thy fhadowes forme,forme happy fhow,
To the cleere day with thy much cleerer light,
When to vn-feeing eyes thy fhade fhines fo?

         How

How would (I say)mine eyes be bleſſed made,
By looking on thee in the liuing day?
When in dead night their faire imperfeſt ſhade,
Through heauy ſleepe on ſightleſſe eyes doth ſtay?
   All dayes are nights to ſee till I ſee thee,
   And nights bright daies when dreams do ſhew thee me,

44

IF the dull ſubſtance of my fleſh were thought,
Iniurious diſtance ſhould not ſtop my way,
For then diſpight of ſpace I would be brought,
From limits farre remote,where thou dooſt ſtay,
No matter then although my foote did ſtand
Vpon the fartheſt earth remoou'd from thee,
For nimble thought can iumpe both ſea and land,
As ſoone as thinke the place where he would be.
But ah,thought kills me that I am not thought
To leape large lengths of miles when thou art gone,
But that ſo much of earth and water wrought,
I muſt attend,times leaſure with my mone.
   Receiuing naughts by elements ſo ſloe,
   But heauie teares,badges of eithers woe.

45

THe other two,ſlight ayre,and purging fire,
Are both with thee,where euer I abide,
The firſt my thought,the other my deſire,
Theſe preſent abſent with ſwift motion ſlide.
For when theſe quicker Elements are gone
In tender Embaſſie of loue to thee,
My life being made of foure,with two alone,
Sinkes downe to death,oppreſt with melancholie.
Vntill liues compoſition be recured,
By thoſe ſwift meſſengers return'd from thee,
Who euen but now come back againe aſſured,
Of their faire health,recounting it to me.
   This told,I ioy,but then no longer glad,
   I ſend them back againe and ſtraight grow ſad.

46

Mine eye and heart are at a mortall warre,
How to deuide the conqueſt of thy ſight,
Mine eye,my heart their pictures ſight would barre,
My heart,mine eye the freeedome of that right,
My heart doth plead that thou in him dooſt lye,
(A cloſet neuer pearſt with chriſtall eyes)
But the defendant doth that plea deny,
And ſayes in him their faire appearance lyes.
To ſide this title is impannelled
A queſt of thoughts,all tennants to the heart,
And by their verdict is determined
The cleere eyes moyitie,and the deare hearts part.
   As thus,mine eyes due is their outward part,
   And my hearts right,their inward loue of heart.

47

BEtwixt mine eye and heart a league is tooke,
And each doth good turnes now vnto the other,
When that mine eye is famiſht for a looke,
Or heart in loue with ſighes himſelfe doth ſmother;
With my loues picture then my eye doth feaſt,
And to the painted banquet bids my heart:
An other time mine eye is my hearts gueſt,
And in his thoughts of loue doth ſhare a part.
So either by thy picture or my loue,
Thy ſeiſe away,are preſent ſtill with me,
For thou nor farther then my thoughts canſt moue,
And I am ſtill with them,and they with thee.
   Or if they ſleepe, thy picture in my ſight
   Awakes my heart,to hearts and eyes delight.

48

HOw carefull was I when I tooke my way,
Each trifle vnder trueſt barres to thruſt,
That to my vſe it might vn-vſed ſtay
From hands of falſehood,in ſure wards of truſt ?
But thou,to whom my iewels trifles are,

                                             Moſt

Most worthy comfort, now my greatest griefe,
Thou best of deerest, and mine onely care,
Art left the prey of euery vulgar theefe.
Thee haue I not lockt vp in any chest,
Saue where thou art not, though I feele thou art,
Within the gentle closure of my brest,
From whence at pleasure thou maist come and part,
 And euen thence thou wilt be stolne I feare,
 For truth prooues theeuish for a prize so deare.

49

A Gainst that time (if euer that time come)
 When I shall see thee frowne on my defects,
When as thy loue hath cast his vtmost summe,
Cauld to that audite by aduis'd respects,
Against that time when thou shalt strangely passe,
And scarcely greete me with that sunne thine eye,
When loue conuerted from the thing it was
Shall reasons finde of setled grauitie.
Against that time do I insconce me here
Within the knowledge of mine owne desart,
And this my hand, against my selfe vpreare,
To guard the lawfull reasons on thy part,
 To leaue poore me, thou hast the strength of lawes,
 Since why to loue, I can alledge no cause.

50

HOw heauie doe I iourney on the way,
 When what I seeke (my wearie trauels end)
Doth teach that ease and that repose to say
Thus farre the miles are measurde from thy friend.
The beast that beares me, tired with my woe,
Plods duly on, to beare that waight in me,
As if by some instinct the wretch did know
His rider lou'd not speed being made from thee:
The bloody spurre cannot prouoke him on,
That some-times anger thrusts into his hide,
Which heauily he answers with a grone,

More sharpe to me then spurring to his side,
  For that same grone doth put this in my mind,
  My greefe lies onward and my ioy behind.

51

THus can my loue excuse the slow offence,
  Of my dull bearer,when from thee I speed,
From where thou art,why shoulld I hast me thence,
Till I returne of posting is noe need.
O what excuse will my poore beast then find,
When swift extremity can seeme but slow,
Then should I spurre though mounted on the wind,
In winged speed no motion shall I know,
Then can no horse with my desire keepe pace,
Therefore desire(of perfects loue being made)
Shall naigh noe dull flesh in his fiery race,
But loue,for loue,thus shall excuse my iade,
  Since from thee going,he went wilfull slow,
  Towards thee ile run,and giue him leaue to goe.

52

SO am I as the rich whose blessed key,
  Can bring him to his sweet vp-locked treasure,
The which he will not eu'ry hower suruay,
For blunting the fine point of seldome pleasure.
Therefore are feasts so sollemne and so rare,
Since sildom comming in the long yeare set,
Like stones of worth they thinly placed are,
Or captaine Iewells in the carconet.
So is the time that keepes you as my chest,
Or as the ward-robe which the robe doth hide,
To make some speciall instant speciall blest,
By new vnfoulding his imprison'd pride.
  Blessed are you whose worthinesse giues skope,
  Being had to tryumph,being lackt to hope.

53

VVHat is your substance,whereof are you made,
  That millions of strange shaddowes on you tend?
                              Since

Since euery one, hath euery one, one shade,
And you but one, can euery shaddow lend:
Describe *Adonis* and the counterfet,
Is poorely immitated after you,
On *Hellens* cheeke all art of beautie set,
And you in *Grecian* tires are painted new:
Speake of the spring, and foyzon of the yeare,
The one doth shaddow of your beautie show,
The other as your bountie doth appeare,
And you in euery blessed shape we know.
   In all externall grace you haue some part,
   But you like none, none you for constant heart.

54

OH how much more doth beautie beautious seeme,
  By that sweet ornament which truth doth giue,
The Rose lookes faire, but fairer we it deeme
For that sweet odor, which doth in it liue:
The Canker bloomes haue full as deepe a die,
As the perfumed tincture of the Roses,
Hang on such thornes, and play as wantonly,
When sommers breath their masked buds disclofes:
But for their virtue only is their show,
They liue vnwoo'd, and vnrespected fade,
Die to themselues. Sweet Roses doe not so,
Of their sweet deathes, are sweetest odors made:
   And so of you, beautious and louely youth,
   When that shall vade, by verse distils your truth.

55

NOt marble, nor the guilded monument,
  Of Princes shall out-liue this powrefull rime,
But you shall shine more bright in these contents
Then vnswept stone, besmeer'd with sluttish time.
When wastefull warre shall *Statues* ouer-turne,
And broiles roote out the worke of masonry,
Nor *Mars* his sword, nor warres quick fire shall burne
The liuing record of your memory.

                        Gainst

Gainst death, and all obliuious emnity
Shall you pace forth, your praise shall stil finde roome,
Euen in the eyes of all posterity
That weare this world out to the ending doome.
  So til the iudgement that your selfe arise,
  You liue in this, and dwell in louers eies.

56

Sweet loue renew thy force, be it not said
Thy edge should blunter be then apetite,
Which, but too daie by feeding is alaied,
To morrow sharpned in his former might.
So loue be thou, although too daie thou fill
Thy hungrie eies, euen till they winck with fulnesse,
Too morrow see againe, and doe not kill
The spirit of Loue, with a perpetual dulnesse:
Let this sad *Intrim* like the Ocean be
Which parts the shore, where two contracted new,
Come daily to the banckes, that when they see
Returne of loue, more blest may be the view.
  As cal it Winter, which being ful of care,
  Makes Sōmers welcome, thrice more wish'd, more rare:

57

Being your slaue what should I doe but tend,
Vpon the houres, and times of your desire?
I haue no precious time at al to spend;
Nor seruices to doe til you require.
Nor dare I chide the world without end houre,
Whilst I (my soueraine) watch the clock for you,
Nor thinke the bitternesse of absence sowre,
VVhen you haue bid your seruant once adieue.
Nor dare I question with my iealious thought,
VVhere you may be, or your affaires suppose,
But like a sad slaue stay and thinke of nought
Saue where you are, how happy you make those.
  So true a foole is loue, that in your Will,
  (Though you doe any thing) he thinkes no ill.

58

58

THat God forbid, that made me first your slaue,
 I should in thought controule your times of pleasure,
Or at your hand th' account of houres to craue,
Being your vassail bound to staie your leisure.
Oh let me suffer(being at your beck)
Th' imprison'd absence of your libertie,
And patience tame,to sufferance bide each check,
Without accusing you of iniury.
Be where you list,your charter is so strong,
That you your selfe may priuiledge your time
To what you will,to you it doth belong,
Your selfe to pardon of selfe-doing crime.
    I am to waite,though waiting so be hell,
    Not blame your pleasure be it ill or well.

59

IF their bee nothing new,but that which is,
 Hath beene before, how are our braines beguild,
Which laboring for inuention beare amisse
The second burthen of a former child ?
Oh that record could with a back-ward looke,
Euen of fiue hundreth courses of the Sunne,
Show me your image in some antique booke,
Since minde at first in carrecter was done.
That I might see what the old world could say,
To this composed wonder of your frame,
Whether we are mended,or where better they,
Or whether reuolution be the same.
    Oh sure I am the wits of former daies,
    To subiects worse haue giuen admiring praise.

60

LIke as the waues make towards the pibled shore,
 So do our minuites hasten to their end,
Each changing place with that which goes before,
In sequent toile all forwards do contend.
Natiuity once in the maine of light.
                    E   Crawls

Crawles to maturity, wherewith being crown'd,
Crooked eclipfes gainft his glory fight,
And time that gaue, doth now his gift confound.
Time doth transfixe the florifh fet on youth,
And delues the paralels in beauties brow,
Feedes on the rarities of natures truth,
And nothing ftands but for his fieth to mow.
    And yet to times in hope, my verfe fhall ftand
    Praifing thy worth, difpight his cruell hand.

61

IS it thy wil, thy Image fhould keepe open
My heauy eie lids to the weary night?
Doft thou defire my flumbers fhould be broken,
While fhadowes like to thee do mocke my fight?
Is it thy fpirit that thou fend'ft from thee
So farre from home into my deeds to prye,
To find out fhames and idle houres in me,
The skope and tenure of thy Ieloufie?
O no, thy loue though much, is not fo great,
It is my loue that keepes mine eie awake,
Mine owne true loue that doth my reft defeat,
To plaie the watch-man euer for thy fake.
    For thee watch I, whilft thou doft wake elfewhere,
    From me farre of, with others all to neere.

62

SInne of felfe-loue poffeffeth al mine eie,
And all my foule, and al my euery part;
And for this finne there is no remedie,
It is fo grounded inward in my heart.
Me thinkes no face fo gratious is as mine,
No fhape fo true, no truth of fuch account,
And for my felfe mine owne worth do define,
As I all other in all worths furmount.
But when my glaffe fhewes me my felfe indeed
Beated and chopt with tand antiquitie,
Mine owne felfe loue quite contrary I read

Selfe

Selfe,so selfe louing were iniquity,
T'is thee(my selfe)that for my selfe I praise,
Painting my age with beauty of thy daies,

63

AGainst my loue shall be as I am now
With times iniurious hand chrusht and ore-worne,
When houres haue dreind his blood and fild his brow
With lines and wrincles,when his youthfull morne
Hath trauaild on to Ages steepie night,
And all those beauties whereof now he's King
Are vanishing,or vanisht out of sight,
Stealing away the treasure of his Spring.
For such a time do I now fortifie
Against confounding Ages cruell knife,
That he shall neuer cut from memory
My sweet loues beauty,though my louers life.
His beautie shall in these blacke lines be seene,
And they shall liue, and he in them still greene.

64

WHen I haue seene by times fell hand defaced
The rich proud cost of outworne buried age,
When sometime loftie towers I see downe rased,
And brasse eternall slaue to mortall rage.
When I haue seene the hungry Ocean gaine
Aduantage on the Kingdome of the shoare,
And the firme soile win of the watry maine,
Increasing store with losse,and losse with store.
When I haue seene such interchange of state,
Or state it selfe confounded, to decay,
Ruine hath taught me thus to ruminate
That Time will come and take my loue away.
This thought is as a death which cannot choose
But weepe to haue,that which it feares to loose.

65

SInce brasse,nor stone,nor earth,nor boundlesse sea,
But sad mortallity ore-swaies their power,

How

269

How with this rage shall beautie hold a plea,
Whose action is no stronger then a flower?
O how shall summers hunny breath hold out,
Against the wrackfull siedge of battring dayes,
When rocks impregnable are not so stoute,
Nor gates of steele so strong but time decayes?
O fearefull meditation, where alack,
Shall times best Iewell from times chest lie hid?
Or what strong hand can hold his swift foote back,
Or who his spoile or beautie can forbid?
  O none, vnlesse this miracle haue might,
  That in black inck my loue may still shine bright.

66

TYr'd with all these for restfull death I cry,
  As to behold desert a begger borne,
And needie Nothing trimd in iollitie,
And purest faith vnhappily forsworne,
And gilded honor shamefully misplast,
And maiden vertue rudely strumpeted,
And right perfection wrongfully disgrac'd,
And strength by limping sway disabled,
And arte made tung-tide by authoritie,
And Folly (Doctor-like) controuling skill,
And simple-Truth miscalde Simplicitie,
And captiue-good attending Captaine ill.
  Tyr'd with all these, from these would I be gone,
  Saue that to dye, I leaue my loue alone.

67

AH wherefore with infection should he liue,
  And with his presence grace impietie,
That sinne by him aduantage should atchiue,
And lace it selfe with his societie?
Why should false painting immitate his cheeke,
And steale dead seeing of his liuing hew?
Why should poore beautie indirectly seeke,
Roses of shaddow, since his Rose is true?

Why

Why should he liue, now nature banckrout is,
Beggerd of blood to blush through liuely vaines,
For she hath no exchecker now but his,
And proud of many, liues vpon his gaines?
  O him she stores, to show what welth she had,
  In daies long since, before these last so bad.

68

THus is his cheeke the map of daies out-worne,
  When beauty liu'd and dy'ed as flowers do now,
Before these bastard signes of faire were borne,
Or durst inhabit on a liuing brow:
Before the goulden tresses of the dead,
The right of sepulchers, were shorne away,
To liue a scond life on second head,
Ere beauties dead fleece made another gay:
In him those holy antique howers are seene,
Without all ornament, it selfe and true,
Making no summer of an others greene,
Robbing no ould to dresse his beauty new,
  And him as for a map doth Nature store,
  To shew faulse Art what beauty was of yore.

69

THose parts of thee that the worlds eye doth view,
  Want nothing that the thought of hearts can mend:
All toungs (the voice of soules) giue thee that end,
Vttring bare truth, euen so as foes Commend.
Their outward thus with outward praise is crownd,
But those same toungs that giue thee so thine owne,
In other accents doe this praise confound
By seeing farther then the eye hath showne.
They looke into the beauty of thy mind,
And that in guesse they measure by thy deeds,
Then churls their thoughts (although their eies were kind)
To thy faire flower ad the rancke smell of weeds,
  But why thy odor matcheth not thy show,
  The solye is this, that thou doest common grow.

E 3   Thas

70

THat thou are blam'd shall not be thy defect,
For slanders marke was euer yet the faire,
The ornament of beauty is suspect,
A Crow that flies in heauens sweetest ayre.
So thou be good,slander doth but approue,
Their worth the greater beeing woo'd of time,
For Canker vice the sweetest buds doth loue,
And thou present'st a pure vnstayined prime.
Thou hast past by the ambush of young daies,
Either not assayld,or victor beeing charg'd,
Yet this thy praise cannot be soe thy praise,
To tye vp enuy,euermore inlarged,
  If some suspect of ill maskt not thy show,
  Then thou alone kingdomes of hearts shouldst owe.

71

NOe Longer mourne for me when I am dead,
Then you shall heare the surly sullen bell
Giue warning to the world that I am fled
From this vile world with vildest wormes to dwell:
Nay if you read this line,remember not,
The hand that writ it,for I loue you so,
That I in your sweet thoughts would be forgot,
If thinking on me then should make you woe.
O if(I say)you looke vpon this verse,
When I (perhaps)compounded am with clay,
Do not so much as my poore name reherse;
But let your loue euen with my life decay.
  Least the wise world should looke into your mone,
  And mocke you with me after I am gon.

72

O Least the world should taske you to recite,
What merit liu'd in me that you should loue
After my death(deare loue)for get me quite,
For you in me can nothing worthy proue.
Vnlesse you would deuise some vertuous lye,

To doe more for me then mine owne defert,
And hang more praife vpon deceafed I,
Then nigard truth would willingly impart:
O leaft your true loue may feeme falce in this,
That you for loue fpeake well of me vntrue,
My name be buried where my body is,
And liue no more to fhame nor me,nor you.

For I am fhamd by that which I bring forth,
And fo fhould you,to loue things nothing worth.

73

THat time of yeeare thou maift in me behold,
  When yellow leaues,or none,or few doe hange
Vpon thofe boughes which fhake againft the could,
Bare rn'wd quiers,where late the fweet birds fang.
In me thou feeft the twi-light of fuch day,
As after Sun-fet fadeth in the Weft,
Which by and by blacke night doth take away,
Deaths fecond felfe that feals vp all in reft.
In me thou feeft the glowing of fuch fire,
That on the afhes of his youth doth lye,
As the death bed,whereon it muft expire,
Confum'd with that which it was nurrifht by.

This thou perceu'ft,which makes thy loue more ftrong,
To loue that well,which thou muft leaue ere long.

74

BVt be contented when that fell areft,
  With out all bayle fhall carry me away,
My life hath in this line fome intereft,
Which for memoriall ftill with thee fhall ftay.
When thou reueweft this,thou doeft reuew,
The very part was confecrate to thee,
The earth can haue but earth,which is his due,
My fpirit is thine the better part of me,
So then thou haft but loft the dregs of life,
The pray of wormes,my body being dead,
The coward conqueft of a wretches knife,

To.

273

To bafe of thee to be remembred,
　　The worth of that,is that which it containes,
　　And that is this, and this with thee remaines.

75

SO are you to my thoughts as food to life,
　　Or as fweet feafon'd fhewers are to the ground;
And for the peace of you I hold fuch ftrife,
As twixt a mifer and his wealth is found.
Now proud as an inioyer,and anon
Doubting the filching age will fteale his treafure,
Now counting beft to be with you alone,
Then betterd that the world may fee my pleafure,
Some-time all ful with feafting on your fight,
And by and by cleane ftarued for a looke,
Poffeffing or purfuing no delight
Saue what is had,or muft from you be tooke.
　　Thus do I pine and furfet day by day,
　　Or gluttoning on all,or all away,

76

VVHy is my verfe fo barren of new pride?
　　So far from variation or quicke change?
Why with the time do I not glance afide
To new found methods,and to compounds ftrange?
Why write I ftill all one,euer the fame,
And keepe inuention in a noted weed,
That euery word doth almoft fel my name,
Shewing their birth,and where they did proceed?
O know fweet loue I alwaies write of you,
And you and loue are ftill my argument:
So all my beft is dreffing old words new,
Spending againe what is already fpent:
　　For as the Sun is daily new and old,
　　So is my loue ftill telling what is told,

77

THy glaffe will fhew thee how thy beauties were,
　　Thy dyall how thy pretious mynuits wafte,

The

The vacant leaues thy mindes imprint will beare,
And of this booke,this learning maist thou taste.
The wrinckles which thy glasse will truly show,
Of mouthed graues will giue thee memorie,
Thou by thy dyals shady stealth maist know,
Times theeuish progresse to eternitie.
Looke what thy memorie cannot containe,
Commit to these waste blacks,and thou shalt finde
Those children nurst,deliuerd from thy braine,
To take a new acquaintance of thy minde.
 These offices,so oft as thou wilt looke,
 Shall profit thee,and much inrich thy booke.

78

SO oft haue I inuok'd thee for my Muse,
 And found such faire assistance in my verse,
As euery *Alien* pen hath got my vse,
And vnder thee their poesie disperse.
Thine eyes,that taught the dumbe on high to sing,
And heauie ignorance aloft to flie,
Haue added fethers to the learneds wing,
And giuen grace a double Maiestie.
Yet be most proud of that which I compile,
Whose influence is thine,and borne of thee,
In others workes thou doost but mend the stile,
And Arts with thy sweete graces graced be.
 But thou art all my art,and doost aduance
 As high as learning,my rude ignorance.

79

WHilst I alone did call vpon thy ayde,
 My verse alone had all thy gentle grace,
But now my gracious numbers are decayde,
And my sick Muse doth giue an other place.
I grant (sweet loue)thy louely argument
Deserues the trauaile of a worthier pen,
Yet what of thee thy Poet doth inuent,
He robs thee of,and payes it thee againe,

F   He

He lends thee vertue, and he stole that word,
From thy behauiour, beautie doth he giue
And found it in thy cheeke: he can affoord
No praise to thee, but what in thee doth liue.
    Then thanke him not for that which he doth say,
    Since what he owes thee, thou thy selfe dooſt pay.

80

O How I faint when I of you do write,
  Knowing a better ſpirit doth vſe your name,
And in the praiſe thereof ſpends all his might,
To make me toung-tide ſpeaking of your fame.
But ſince your worth (wide as the Ocean is)
The humble as the proudeſt ſaile doth beare,
My ſawſie barke (inferior farre to his)
On your broad maine doth wilfully appeare.
Your ſhalloweſt helpe will hold me vp a floate,
Whilſt he vpon your ſoundleſſe deepe doth ride,
Or (being-wrackt) I am a worthleſſe bote,
He of tall building, and of goodly pride.
    Then If he thriue and I be caſt away,
    The worſt was this, my loue was my decay.

81

O R I ſhall liue your Epitaph to make,
  Or you ſuruiue when I in earth am rotten,
From hence your memory death cannot take,
Although in me each part will be forgotten.
Your name from hence immortall life ſhall haue,
Though I (once gone) to all the world muſt dye,
The earth can yeeld me but a common graue,
When you intombed in mens eyes ſhall lye,
Your monument ſhall be my gentle verſe,
Which eyes not yet created ſhall ore-read,
And toungs to be, your beeing ſhall rehearſe,
When all the breathers of this world are dead,
    You ſtill ſhall liue (ſuch vertue hath my Pen)
    Where breath moſt breaths, euen in the mouths of men.

I grant

82

I Grant thou wert not married to my Muſe,
  And therefore maieſt without attaint ore-looke
The dedicated words which writers vſe
Of their faire ſubiect,bleſſing euery booke.
Thou art as faire in knowledge as in hew,
Finding thy worth a limmit paſt my praiſe,
And therefore art inforc'd to ſeeke anew,
Some freſher ſtampe of the time bettering dayes.
And do ſo loue,yet when they haue deuiſde,
What ſtrained touches Rhethorick can lend,
Thou truly faire,wert truly ſimpathizde,
In true plaine words,by thy true telling friend.
    And their groſſe painting might be better vſ'd,
    Where cheekes need blood,in thee it is abuſ'd.

83

I Neuer ſaw that you did painting need,
  And therefore to your faire no painting ſet,
I found (or thought I found) you did exceed,
The barren tender of a Poets debt:
And therefore haue I ſlept in your report,
That you your ſelfe being extant well might ſhow,
How farre a moderne quill doth come to ſhort,
Speaking of worth,what worth in you doth grow,
This ſilence for my ſinne you did impute,
Which ſhall be moſt my glory being dombe,
For I impaire not beautie being mute,
When others would giue life,and bring a tombe.
    There liues more life in one of your faire eyes,
    Then both your Poets can in praiſe deuiſe.

84

WHo is it that ſayes moſt,which can ſay more,
   Then this rich praiſe,that you alone,are you,
In whoſe confine immured is the ſtore,
Which ſhould example where your equall grew,
Leane penurie within that Pen doth dwell,

F 2   That

That to his subiect lends not some small glory,
But he that writes of you,if he can tell,
That you are you,so dignifies his story.
Let him but coppy what in you is writ,
Not making worse what nature made so cleere,
And such a counter-part shall fame his wit,
Making his stile admired euery where.
   You to your beautious blessings adde a curse,
   Being fond on praise,which makes your praises worse.

85

MY toung-tide Muse in manners holds her still,
  While comments of your praise richly compil'd,
Reserue their Character with goulden quill,
And precious phrase by all the Muses fil'd.
I thinke good thoughts,whilst other write good wordes,
And like vnlettered clarke still crie Amen,
To euery Himne that able spirit affords,
In polisht forme of well refined pen.
Hearing you praisd,I say 'tis so, 'tis true,
And to the most of praise adde some-thing more,
But that is in my thought,whose loue to you
(Though words come hind-most)holds his ranke before,
   Then others,for the breath of words respect,
   Me for my dombe thoughts,speaking in effect.

86

VVAs it the proud full saile of his great verse,
  Bound for the prize of (all to precious) you,
That did my ripe thoughts in my braine inhearce,
Making their tombe the wombe wherein they grew?
Was it his spirit,by spirits taught to write,
Aboue a mortall pitch,that struck me dead?
No,neither he,nor his compiers by night
Giuing him ayde,my verse astonished.
He nor that affable familiar ghost
Which nightly gulls him with intelligence,
As victors of my silence cannot boast,

                                       I was

I was not sick of any feare from thence,
　But when your countinance fild vp his line,
　Then lackt I matter, that infeebled mine.

87

FArewell thou art too deare for my possessing,
　And like enough thou knowst thy estimate,
The Cha ter of thy worth giues thee releasing:
My bonds in thee are all determinate.
For how do I hold thee but by thy granting,
And for that ritches where is my deseruing?
The cause of this faire guift in me is wanting,
And so my pattent back againe is sweruing.
Thy selfe thou gau'st, thy owne worth then not knowing,
Or mee to whom thou gau'st it, else mistaking,
So thy great guift vpon misprision growing,
Comes home againe, on better iudgement making.
　Thus haue I had thee as a dreame doth flatter,
　In sleepe a King, but waking no such matter.

88

VVHen thou shalt be dispode to set me light,
　And place my merrit in the eie of skorne,
Vpon thy side, against my selfe ile fight,
And proue thee virtuous, though thou art forsworne:
With mine owne weakenesse being best acquainted,
Vpon thy part I can set downe a story
Of faults conceald, wherein I am attainted:
That thou in loosing me, shall win much glory:
And I by this wil be a gainer too,
For bending all my louing thoughts on thee,
The iniuries that to my selfe I doe,
Doing thee vantage, duble vantage me.
　Such is my loue, to thee I so belong,
　That for thy right, my selfe will beare all wrong.

89

SAy that thou didst forsake mee for some falt,
　And I will comment vpon that offence,

F 3

The

Speake of my lamenesse, and I straight will halt:
Against thy reasons making no defence.
Thou canst not(loue)disgrace me halfe so ill,
To set a forme vpon desired change,
As ile my selfe disgrace,knowing thy wil,
I will acquaintance strangle and looke strange:
Be absent from thy walkes and in my tongue,
Thy sweet beloued name no more shall dwell,
Least I(too much proface)should do it wronge:
And haplie of our old acquaintance tell.
   For thee,against my selfe ile vow debate,
   For I must nere loue him whom thou dost hate.

90

THen hate me when thou wilt, if euer,now,
  Now while the world is bent my deeds to crosse,
Ioyne with the spight of fortune,make me bow,
And doe not drop in for an after losse:
Ah doe not,when my heart hath scapte this sorrow,
Come in the rereward of a conquerd woe,
Giue not a windy night a rainie morrow,
To linger out a purposd ouer-throw.
If thou wilt leaue me, do not leaue me last,
When other pettie griefes haue done their spight,
But in the onset come,so stall I taste
At first the very worst of fortunes might.
   And other straines of woe, which now seeme woe,
   Compar'd with losse of thee,will not seeme so.

91

SOme glory in their birth,some in their skill,
  Some in their wealth,some in their bodies force,
Some in their garments though new-fangled ill:
Some in their Hawkes and Hounds,some in their Horse.
And euery humor hath his adiunct pleasure,
Wherein it findes a ioy aboue the rest,
But these perticulers are not my measure,
All these I better in one generall best.

                      Thy

Thy loue is bitter then high birth to me,
Richer then wealth, prouder then garments cost,
Of more delight then Hawkes or Horses bee:
And hauing thee, of all mens pride I boast.
    Wretched in this alone, that thou maist take,
    All this away, and me most wretched make.

92

BVt doe thy worst to steale thy selfe away,
  For tearme of life thou art assured mine,
And life no longer then thy loue will stay,
For it depends vpon that loue of thine.
Then need I not to feare the worst of wrongs,
When in the least of them my life hath end,
I see, a better state to me belongs
Then that, which on thy humor doth depend.
Thou canst not vex me with inconstant minde,
Since that my life on thy reuolt doth lie,
Oh what a happy title do I finde,
Happy to haue thy loue, happy to die!
    But whats so blessed faire that feares no blot,
    Thou maist be falce, and yet I know it not.

93

SO shall I liue, supposing thou art true,
  Like a deceiued husband, so loues face,
May still seeme loue to me, though alter'd new:
Thy lookes with me, thy heart in other place.
For their can liue no hatred in thine eye,
Therefore in that I cannot know thy change,
In manies lookes, the falce hearts history
Is writ in moods and frounes and wrinckles strange.
But heauen in thy creation did decree,
That in thy face sweet loue should euer dwell,
What ere thy thoughts, or thy hearts workings be,
Thy lookes should nothing thence, but sweetnesse tell.
    How like *Eaues* apple doth thy beauty grow,
    If thy sweet vertue answere not thy show.

94

94

THey that haue powre to hurt, and will doe none,
That doe not do the thing, they moſt do ſhowe,
Who mouing others, are themſelues as ſtone,
Vnmooued, could, and to temptation ſlow:
They rightly do inherrit heauens graces,
And husband natures ritches from expence,
They are the Lords and owners of their faces,
Others, but ſtewards of their excellence:
The ſommers flowre is to the ſommer ſweet,
Though to it ſelfe, it onely liue and die,
But if that flowre with baſe infection meete,
The baſeſt weed out-braues his dignity:
　　For ſweeteſt things turne ſowreſt by their deedes,
　　Lillies that feſter, ſmell far worſe then weeds.

95

HOw ſweet and louely doſt thou make the ſhame,
Which like a canker in the fragrant Roſe,
Doth ſpot the beautie of thy budding name?
Oh in what ſweets doeſt thou thy ſinnes incloſe!
That tongue that tells the ſtory of thy daies,
(Making laſciuious comments on thy ſport)
Cannot diſpraiſe, but in a kinde of praiſe,
Naming thy name, bleſſes an ill report.
Oh what a manſion haue thoſe vices got,
Which for their habitation choſe out thee,
Where beauties vaile doth couer euery blot,
And all things turnes to faire, that eies can ſee!
　　Take heed (deare heart) of this large priuiledge,
　　The hardeſt kniſe ill vſ'd doth looſe his edge.

96

SOme ſay thy fault is youth, ſome wantoneſſe,
Some ſay thy grace is youth and gentle ſport,
Both grace and faults are lou'd of more and leſſe:
Thou makſt faults graces, that to thee reſort:
As on the finger of a throned Queene,

The

The basest Iewell wil be well esteem'd:
So are those errors that in thee are seene,
To truths translated,and for true things deem'd.
How many Lambs might the sterne Wolfe betray,
If like a Lambe he could his lookes translate.
How many gazers mighst thou lead away,
If thou wouldst vse the strength of all thy state?
   But doe not so,I loue thee in such sort,
   As thou being mine,mine is thy good report.

97

HOw like a Winter hath my absence beene
From thee,the pleasure of the fleeting yeare?
   What freezings haue I felt,what darke daies seene?
What old Decembers barenesse euery where?
And yet this time remou'd was sommers time,
The teeming Autumne big with ritch increase,
Bearing the wanton burthen of the prime,
Like widdowed wombes after their Lords decease:
Yet this aboundant issue seem'd to me,
But hope of Orphans,and vn-fathered fruite,
For Sommer and his pleasures waite on thee,
And thou away,the very birds are mute.
   Or if they sing,tis with so dull a cheere,
   That leaues looke pale,dreading the Winters neere.

98

FRom you haue I beene absent in the spring,
When proud pide Aprill (drest in all his trim)
Hath put a spirit of youth in euery thing:
That heauie Saturne laught and leapt with him.
Yet nor the laies of birds,nor the sweet smell
Of different flowers in odor and in hew,
Could make me any summers story tell:
Or from their proud lap pluck them where they grew:
Nor did I wonder at the Lillies white,
Nor praise the deepe vermillion in the Rose,
They weare but sweet,but figures of delight:

G

Drawne

Drawne after you, you patterne of all those.
   Yet seem'd it Winter still, and you away,
   As with your shaddow I with these did play.

99

THe forward violet thus did I chide,
   Sweet theefe whence didst thou steale thy sweet that
If not from my loues breath, the purple pride,   (smels
Which on thy soft cheeke for complexion dwells?
In my loues veines thou hast too grosely died,
The Lillie I condemned for thy hand,
And buds of marierom had stolne thy haire,
The Roses fearefully on thornes did stand,
Our blushing shame, an other white dispaire:
A third nor red, nor white, had stolne of both,
And to his robbry had annext thy breath,
But for his theft in pride of all his growth
A vengfull canker eate him vp to death.
   More flowers I noted, yet I none could see,
   But sweet, or culler it had stolne from thee.

100

VVHere art thou Muse that thou forgetst so long,
   To speake of that which giues thee all thy might?
Spendst thou thy furie on some worthlesse songe,
Darkning thy powre to lend base subiects light.
Returne forgetfull Muse, and straight redeeme,
In gentle numbers time so idely spent,
Sing to the eare that doth thy laies esteeme,
And giues thy pen both skill and argument.
Rise resty Muse, my loues sweet face suruay,
If time haue any wrincle grauen there,
If any, be a *Satire* to decay,
And make times spoiles dispised euery where.
   Giue my loue fame faster then time wasts life,
   So thou preuenst his sieth, and crooked knife.

101

OH truant Muse what shalbe thy amends,

For thy neglect of truth in beauty di'd?
Both truth and beauty on my loue depends:
So doſt thou too,and therein dignifi'd:
Make anſwere Muſe,wilt thou not haply ſaie,
Truth needs no collour with his collour fixt,
Beautie no penſell,beauties truth to lay:
But beſt is beſt,if neuer intermixt.
Becauſe he needs no praiſe,wilt thou be dumb?
Excuſe not ſilence ſo,for't lies in thee,
To make him much out-liue a gilded tombe:
And to be praiſd of ages yet to be.
 Then do thy office Muſe,I teach thee how,
 To make him ſeeme long hence,as he ſhowes now.

102

MY loue is ſtrengthned though more weake in ſee-
I loue not leſſe,thogh leſſe the ſhow appeare, (ming
That loue is marchandiz'd,whoſe ritch eſteeming,
The owners tongue doth publiſh euery where.
Our loue was new,and then but in the ſpring,
When I was wont to greet it with my laies,
As *Philomell* in ſummers front doth ſinge,
And ſtops his pipe in growth of riper daies:
Not that the ſummer is leſſe pleaſant now
Then when her mournefull himns did huſh the night,
But that wild muſick burthens euery bow,
And ſweets growne common looſe their deare delight.
 Therefore like her,I ſome-time hold my tongue:
 Becauſe I would not dull you with my ſonge.

103

A Lack what pouerty my Muſe brings forth,
That hauing ſuch a skope to ſhow her pride,
The argument all bare is of more worth
Then when it hath my added praiſe beſide.
Oh blame me not if I no more can write!
Looke in your glaſſe and there appeares a face,
That ouer-goes my blunt inuention quite,
Dulling my lines,and doing me diſgrace.
   G 2   Were

Were it not sinfull then striuing to mend,
To marre the subiect that before was well,
For to no other passe my verses tend,
Then of your graces and your gifts to tell.
　And more,inuch more then in my verse can sit,
　Your owne glasse showes you,when you looke in it.

104

TO me faire friend you neuer can be old,
　For as you were when first your eye I eyde,
Such seemes your beautie still:Three Winters colde,
Haue from the forrests shooke three summers pride,
Three beautious springs to yellow *Autumne* turn'd,
In processe of the seasons haue I seene,
Three Aprill perfumes in three hot Iunes burn'd,
Since first I saw you fresh which yet are greene.
Ah yet doth beauty like a Dyall hand,
Steale from his figure,and no pace perceiu'd,
So your sweete hew,which me thinkes still doth stand
Hath motion,and mine eye may be deceaued.
　For feare of which,heare this thou age vnbred,
　Ere you were borne was beauties summer dead.

105

LEt not my loue be cal'd Idolatrie,
　Nor my beloued as an Idoll show,
Since all alike my songs and praises be
To one,of one,still such,and euer so.
Kinde is my loue to day,to morrow kinde,
Still constant in a wondrous excellence,
Therefore my verse to constancie confin'de,
One thing expressing,leaues out difference.
Faire,kinde,and true,is all my argument,
Faire,kinde and true,varrying to other words,
And in this change is my inuencion spent,
Three theams in one,which wondrous scope affords.
　Faire,kinde,and true,haue often liu'd alone.
　Which three till now,neuer kept seate in one.

When

106

WHen in the Chronicle of wasted time,
I see discriptions of the fairest wights,
And beautie making beautifull old rime,
In praise of Ladies dead, and louely Knights,
Then in the blazon of sweet beauties best,
Of hand, of foote, of lip, of eye, of brow,
I see their antique Pen would haue exprest,
Euen such a beauty as you maister now.
So all their praises are but prophesies
Of this our time, all you prefiguring,
And for they look'd but with deuining eyes,
They had not still enough your worth to sing:
    For we which now behold these present dayes,
    Haue eyes to wonder, but lack toungs to praise.

107

NOt mine owne feares, nor the prophetick soule,
Of the wide world, dreaming on things to come,
Can yet the lease of my true loue controule,
Supposde as forfeit to a confin'd doome.
The mortall Moone hath her eclipse indur'de,
And the sad Augurs mock their owne presage,
Incertenties now crowne them-selues assur'de,
And peace proclaimes Oliues of endlesse age.
Now with the drops of this most balmie time,
My loue lookes fresh, and death to me subscribes,
Since spight of him Ile liue in this poore rime,
While he insults ore dull and speachlesse tribes.
    And thou in this shalt finde thy monument,
    When tyrants crests and tombs of brasse are spent.

108

VVHat's in the braine that Inck may character,
Which hath not figur'd to thee my true spirit,
What's new to speake, what now to register,
That may expresse my loue, or thy deare merit?
Nothing sweet boy, but yet like prayers diuine,

G 3   I must

I muſt each day ſay ore the very ſame,
Counting no old thing old,thou mine,I thine,
Euen as when firſt I hallowed thy faire name.
So that eternall loue in loues freſh caſe,
Waighes not the duſt and iniury of age,
Nor giues to neceſſary wrinckles place,
But makes antiquitie for aye his page,
  Finding the firſt conceit of loue there bred,
  Where time and outward forme would ſhew it dead,

109

O Neuer ſay that I was falſe of heart,
  Though abſence ſeem'd my flame to quallifie,
As eaſie might I from my ſelfe depart,
As from my ſoule which in thy breſt doth lye:
That is my home of loue, if I haue rang'd,
Like him that trauels I returne againe,
Iuſt to the time,not with the time exchang'd,
So that my ſelfe bring water for my ſtaine,
Neuer beleeue though in my nature raign'd,
All frailties that beſiege all kindes of blood,
That it could ſo prepoſterouſlie be ſtain'd,
To leaue for nothing all thy ſumme of good :
  For nothing this wide Vniuerſe I call,
  Saue thou my Roſe,in it thou art my all.

110

A Las 'tis true,I haue gone here and there,
  And made my ſelfe a motley to the view,
Gor'd mine own thoughts, ſold cheap what is moſt deare,
Made old offences of affections new.
Moſt true it is,that I haue lookt on truth
Aſconce and ſtrangely: But by all aboue,
Theſe blenches gaue my heart an other youth,
And worſe eſſaies prou'd thee my beſt of loue,
Now all is done,haue what ſhall haue no end,
Mine appetite I neuer more will grin'de
On newer proofe,to trie an older friend,
A God in loue,to whom I am confin'd.

Then

288

Then giue me welcome,next my heauen the beſt,
Euen to thy pure and moſt moſt louing breſt.

111

OFor my ſake doe you wiſh fortune chide,
The guiltie goddeſſe of my harmfull deeds,
That did not better for my life prouide,
Then publick meanes which publick manners breeds.
Thence comes it that my name receiues a brand,
And almoſt thence my nature is ſubdu'd
To what it workes in,like the Dyers hand,
Pitty me then,and wiſh I were renu'de;
Whilſt like a willing pacient I will drinke,
Potions of Eyſell gainſt my ſtrong infection,
No bitterneſſe that I will bitter thinke,
Nor double pennance to correct correction.
    Pittie me then deare friend,and I aſſure yee,
    Euen that your pittie is enough to cure mee.

112

YOur loue and pittie doth th'impreſſion fill,
Which vulgar ſcandall ſtampt vpon my brow,
For what care I who calles me well or ill,
So you ore-greene my bad,my good alow?
You are my All the world,and I muſt ſtriue,
To know my ſhames and praiſes from your tounge,
None elſe to me,nor I to none aliue,
That my ſteel'd ſence or changes right or wrong,
In ſo profound *Abiſme* I throw all care
Of others voyces,that my Adders ſence,
To cryttick and to flatterer ſtopped are:
Marke how with my neglect I doe diſpence.
    You are ſo ſtrongly in my purpoſe bred,
    That all the world beſides me thinkes y'are dead.

113

SInce I left you,mine eye is in my minde,
And that which gouernes me to goe about,
Doth part his function,and is partly blind,

                                    Seemes

Seemes feeing,but effectually is out:
For it no forme deliuers to the heart
Of bird,of flowre,or fhape which it doth lack,
Of his quick obiects hath the minde no part,
Nor his owne vifion houlds what it doth catch:
For if it fee the rud'ft or gentleft fight,
The moft fweet-fauor or deformedft creature,
The mountaine,or the fea,the day,or night:
The Croe,or Doue,it fhapes them to your feature.
  Incapable of more repleat,with you,
  My moft true minde thus maketh mine vntrue.

114

OR whether doth my minde being crown'd with you
  Drinke vp the monarks plague this flattery?
Or whether fhall I fay mine eie faith true,
And that your loue taught it this *Alcumie?*
To make of monfters,and things indigeft,
Such cherubines as your fweet felfe refemble,
Creating euery bad a perfect beft
As faft as obiects to his beames affemble:
Oh tis the firft,tis flatry in my feeing,
And my great minde moft kingly drinkes it vp,
Mine eie well knowes what with his guft is greeing,
And to his pallat doth prepare the cup.
  If it be poifon'd,tis the leffer finne,
  That mine eye loues it and doth firft beginne.

115

THofe lines that I before haue writ doe lie,
  Euen thofe that faid I could not loue you deerer,
Yet then my iudgement knew no reafon why,
My moft full flame fhould afterwards burne cleerer.
But reckening time,whofe milliond accidents
Creepe in twixt vowes,and change decrees of Kings,
Tan facred beautie,blunt the fharp'ft intents,
Diuert ftrong mindes to th' courfe of altring things:
Alas why fearing of times tiranie,

Might

Might I not then say now I loue you best,
When I was certaine ore in-certainty,
Crowning the present,doubting of the rest:
  Loue is a Babe, then might I not say so
  To giue full growth to that which still doth grow.

119

LEt me not to the marriage of true mindes
  Admit impediments,loue is not loue
Which alters when it alteration findes,
Or bends with the remouer to remoue.
O no,it is an euer fixed marke
That lookes on tempests and is neuer shaken;
It is the star to euery wandring barke,
Whose worths vnknowne,although his higth be taken.
Lou's not Times foole,though rosie lips and cheeks
Within his bending sickles compasse come,
Loue alters not with his breefe houres and weekes,
But beares it out euen to the edge of doome:
  If this be error and vpon me proued,
  I neuer writ,nor no man euer loued.

117

ACcuse me thus,that I haue scanted all,
  Wherein I should your great deserts repay,
Forgot vpon your dearest loue to call,
Whereto al bonds do tie me day by day,
That I haue frequent binne with vnknown mindes,
And giuen to time your owne deare purchas'd right,
That I haue hoysted saile to al the windes
Which should transport me farthest from your sight.
Booke both my wilfulnesse and errors downe,
And on iust proofe surmise,accumilate,
Bring me within the leuel of your frowne,
But shoote not at me in your wakened hate:
  Since my appeale saies I did striue to prooue
  The constancy and virtue of your loue

H

118

Like as to make our appetites more keene
With eager compounds we our pallat vrge,
As to preuent our malladies vnseene,
We ficken to fhun fickneffe when we purge.
Euen fo being full of your nere cloying fweetneffe,
To bitter fawces did I frame my feeding;
And ficke of wel-fare found a kind of meetneffe,
To be difeaf'd ere that there was true needing.
Thus pollicie in loue t'anticipate
The ills that were, not grew to faults affured,
And brought to medicine a healthfull ftate
Which rancke of goodneffe would by ill be cured.
    But thence I learne and find the leffon true,
    Drugs poyfon him that fo fell ficke of you.

119

What potions haue I drunke of *Syren* teares
Diftil'd from Lymbecks foule as hell within,
Applying feares to hopes, and hopes to feares,
Still loofing when I faw my felfe to win?
What wretched errors hath my heart committed,
Whilft it hath thought it felfe fo bleffed neuer?
How haue mine eies out of their Spheares bene fitted
In the diftraction of this madding feuer?
O benefit of ill, now I find true
That better is, by euil ftill made better.
And ruin'd loue when it is built anew
Growes fairer then at firft, more ftrong, far greater.
    So I returne rebukt to my content,
    And gaine by ills thrife more then I haue fpent.

120

That you were once vnkind be-friends mee now,
And for that forrow, which I then didde feele,
Needes muft I vnder my tranfgreffion bow,
Vnleffe my Nerues were braffe or hammered fteele.
For if you were by my vnkindneffe fhaken

As I by yours , y'haue paſt a hell of Time,
And I a tyrant haue no leaſure taken
To waigh how once I ſuffered in your crime.
O that our night of wo might haue remembred
My deepeſt ſence, how hard true ſorrow hits,
And ſoone to you, as you to me then tendred
The humble ſalue, which wounded boſomes fits!
    But that your treſpaſſe now becomes a fee,
    Mine ranſoms yours, and yours muſt ranſome mee.

121

TIS better to be vile then vile eſteemed,
   When not to be, receiues reproach of being,
And the iuſt pleaſure loſt, which is ſo deemed,
Not by our feeling, but by others ſecing.
For why ſhould others falſe adulterat eyes
Giue ſalutation to my ſportiue blood?
Or on my frailties why are frailer ſpies;
Which in their wils count bad what I think good?
Noe, I am that I am, and they that leuell
At my abuſes, reckon vp their owne,
I may be ſtraight though they them-ſelues be beuel
By their rancke thoughtes, my deedes muſt not be ſhown
    Vnleſſe this generall euill they maintaine,
    All men are bad and in their badneſſe raigne.

122.

THy guiſt, thy tables, are within my braine
   Full characterd with laſting memory,
Which ſhall aboue that idle rancke remaine
Beyond all date euen to eternity.
Or at the leaſt, ſo long as braine and heart
Haue facultie by nature to ſubſiſt,
Til each to raz'd obliuion yeeld his part,
Of thee, thy record neuer can be miſt.
That poore retention could not ſo much hold,
Nor need I tallies thy deare loue to skore,
Therefore to giue them from me was I bold,

To truſt thoſe tables that receaue thee more,
To keepe an adiunckt to remember thee,
Were to import forgetfulneſſe in mee.

133

NO! Time, thou ſhalt not boſt that I doe change,
Thy pyramyds buylt vp with newer might
To me are nothing nouell, nothing ſtrange,
They are but dreſſings of a former ſight:
Our dates are breefe, and therefor we admire,
What thou doſt foyſt vpon vs that is ould,
And rather make them borne to our deſire,
Then thinke that we before haue heard them tould:
Thy regiſters and thee I both defie,
Not wondring at the preſent, nor the paſt,
For thy records, and what we ſee doth lye,
Made more or les by thy continuall haſt:
    This I doe vow and this ſhall euer be,
    I will be true diſpight thy ſyeth and thee.

124

YF my deare loue were but the childe of ſtate,
It might for fortunes baſterd be vnfathered,
As ſubiect to times loue, or to times hate,
Weeds among weeds, or flowers with flowers gatherd.
No it was buylded far from accident,
It ſuffers not in ſmilinge pomp, nor falls
Vnder the blow of thralled diſcontent,
Whereto th'inuiting time our faſhion calls:
It feares not policy that *Heriticke*,
Which workes on leaſes of ſhort numbred howers,
But all alone ſtands hugely pollitick,
That it nor growes with heat, nor drownes with ſhowres.
    To this I witnes call the foles of time,
    Which die for goodnes, who haue liu'd for crime.

125

VVEr't ought to me I bore the canopy,
With my extern the outward honoring,

Or

Or layd great bafes for eternity,
Which proues more fhort then waft or ruining?
Haue I not feene dwellers on forme and fauor
Lofe all, and more by paying too much rent
For compound fweet; Forgoing fimple fauor,
Pittifull thriuors in their gazing fpent.
Noe, let me be obfequious in thy heart,
And take thou my oblacion, poore but free,
Which is not mixt with feconds, knows no art,
But mutuall render, onely me for thee.
  Hence, thou fubbornd *Informer*, a trew foule
  When moft impeacht, ftands leaft in thy controule.

126

O Thou my louely Boy who in thy power,
  Doeft hould times fickle glaffe, his fickle, hower:
Who haft by wayning growne, and therein fhou'ft,
Thy louers withering, as thy fweet felfe grow'ft.
If Nature (foueraine mifteres ouer wrack)
As thou goeft onwards ftill will plucke thee backe,
She keepes thee to this purpofe, that her skill.
May time difgrace, and wretched mynuit kill.
Yet feare her O thou minnion of her pleafure,
She may detaine, but not ftill keepe her trefure!
Her *Audite* (though delayd) anfwer'd muft be,
And her *Quietus* is to render thee.
       (   )
       (   )

127

IN the ould age blacke was not counted faire,
  Or if it weare it bore not beauties name:
But now is blacke beauties fucceffiue heire,
And Beautie flanderd with a baftard fhame,
For fince each hand hath put on Natures power,
Fairing the foule with Arts faulfe borrow'd face,
Sweet beauty hath no name no holy boure,
But is prophan'd, if not liues in difgrace.

H 3

Therefore.

Therefore my Mistersse eyes are Rauen blacke,
Her eyes so suted, and they mourners seeme,
At such who not borne faire no beauty lack,
Slandring Creation with a false esteeme,
    Yet so they mourne becomming of their woe,
    That euery toung saies beauty should looke so.

128

HOw oft when thou my musike musike playst,
  Vpon that blessed wood whose motion sounds
With thy sweet fingers when thou gently swayst,
The wiry concord that mine eare confounds,
Do I enuie those Iackes that nimble leape,
To kisse the tender inward of thy hand,
Whilst my poore lips which should that haruest reape,
At the woods bouldnes by thee blushing stand.
To be so tikled they would change their state,
And situation with those dancing chips,
Ore whome their fingers walke with gentle gate,
Making dead wood more blest then liuing lips,
    Since sausie Iackes so happy are in this,
    Giue them their fingers, me thy lips to kisse.

129

TH'expence of Spirit in a waste of shame
  Is lust in action, and till action, lust
Is periurd, murdrous, blouddy full of blame,
Sauage, extreame, rude, cruell, not to trust,
Inioyd no sooner but dispised straight,
Past reason hunted, and no sooner had
Past reason hated as a swollowed bayt,
On purpose layd to make the taker mad.
Made In pursut and in possession so,
Had, hauing, and in quest, to haue extreame,
A blisse in proofe and proud and very wo,
Before a ioy propos'd behind a dreame,
    All this the world well knowes yet none knowes well,
    To shun the heauen that leads men to this hell.

My

130

MY Miſtres eyes are nothing like the Sunne,
Currall is farre more red,then her lips red,
If ſnow be white,why then her breſts are dun:
If haires be wiers,black wiers grow on her head:
I haue ſeene Roſes damaskt,red and white,
But no ſuch Roſes ſee I in her cheekes,
And in ſome perfumes is there more delight,
Then in the breath that from my Miſtres reekes.
I loue to heare her ſpeake,yet well I know,
That Muſicke hath a farre more pleaſing ſound:
I graunt I neuer ſaw a goddeſſe goe,
My Miſtres when ſhee walkes treads on the ground,
　　And yet by heauen I thinke my loue as rare,
　　As any ſhe beli'd with falſe compare.

131

THou art as tiranous,ſo as thou art,
As thoſe whoſe beauties proudly make them cruell;
For well thou know'ſt to my deare doting hart
Thou art the faireſt and moſt precious Iewell.
Yet in good faith ſome ſay that thee behold,
Thy face hath not the power to make loue grone;
To ſay they erre,I dare not be ſo bold,
Although I ſweare it to my ſelfe alone.
And to be ſure that is not falſe I ſweare
A thouſand grones but thinking on thy face,
One on anothers necke do witneſſe beare
Thy blacke is faireſt in my iudgements place.
　　In nothing art thou blacke ſaue in thy deeds,
　　And thence this ſlaunder as I thinke proceeds.

132

THine eies I loue,and they as pittying me,
Knowing thy heart torment me with diſdaine,
Haue put on black,and louing mourners bee,
Looking with pretty ruth vpon my paine.

And

And truly not the morning Sun of Heauen
Better becomes the gray cheeks of th'Eaſt,
Nor that full Starre that vſhers in the Eauen
Doth halfe that glory to the ſober Weſt
As thoſe two morning eyes become thy face:
O let it then as well beſeeme thy heart
To mourne for me ſince mourning doth thee grace,
And ſute thy pitty like in euery part.
　Then will I ſweare beauty her ſelfe is blacke,
　And all they foule that thy complexion lacke.

133

BEſhrew that heart that makes my heart to groane
For that deepe wound it giues my friend and me;
I'ſt not ynough to torture me alone,
But ſlaue to ſlauery my ſweet'ſt friend muſt be.
Me from my ſelfe thy cruell eye hath taken,
And my next ſelfe thou harder haſt ingroſſed,
Of him,my ſelfe,and thee I am forſaken,
A torment thrice three-fold thus to be croſſed :
Priſon my heart in thy ſteele boſomes warde,
But then my friends heart let my poore heart bale,
Who ere keepes me,let my heart be his garde,
Thou canſt not then vſe rigor in my Iaile.
　And yet thou wilt,for I being pent in thee,
　Perforce am thine and all that is in me.

134

SO now I haue confeſt that he is thine,
And I my ſelfe am morgag'd to thy will,
My ſelfe Ile forfeit,ſo that other mine,
Thou wilt reſtore to be my comfort ſtill:
But thou wilt not,nor he will not be free,
For thou art couetous,and he is kinde,
He learnd but ſuretie-like to write for me,
Vnder that bond that him as faſt doth binde.
The ſtatute of thy beauty thou wilt take,
Thou vſurer that put'ſt forth all to vſe,

And

And ſue a friend, came debter for my ſake,
So him I looſe through my vnkinde abuſe.
  Him haue I loſt, thou haſt both him and me,
  He paies the whole, and yet am I not free.

135

WHo euer hath her wiſh, thou haſt thy *Will*,
  And *will* too boote, and *Will* in ouer-plus,
More then enough am I that vexe thee ſtill,
To thy ſweet will making addition thus.
Wilt thou whoſe will is large and ſpatious,
Not once vouchſafe to hide my will in thine,
Shall will in others ſeeme right gracious,
And in my will no faire acceptance ſhine:
The ſea all water, yet receiues raine ſtill,
And in aboundance addeth to his ſtore,
So thou beeing rich in *Will* adde to thy *Will*,
One will of mine to make thy large *Will* more.
  Let no vnkinde, no faire beſeechers kill,
  Thinke all but one, and me in that one *Will*.

136

IF thy ſoule check thee that I come ſo neere,
  Sweare to thy blind ſoule that I was thy *Will*,
And will thy ſoule knowes is admitted there,
Thus farre for loue, my loue-ſute ſweet fullfill.
Will, will fulfill the treaſure of thy loue,
I fill it full with wils, and my will one,
In things of great receit with eaſe we prooue.
Among a number one is reckon'd none.
Then in the number let me paſſe vntold,
Though in thy ſtores account I one muſt be,
For nothing hold me, ſo it pleaſe thee hold,
That nothing me, a ſome-thing ſweet to thee.
  Make but my name thy loue, and loue that ſtill,
  And then thou loueſt me for my name is *Will*.

137

THou blinde foole loue, what dooſt thou to mine eyes,

I   That

That they behold and fee not what they fee:
They know what beautie is,fee where it lyes,
Yet what the beft is,take the worft to be.
If eyes corrupt by ouer-partiall lookes,
Be anchord in the baye where all men ride,
Why of eyes falfehood haft thou forged hookes,
Whereto the iudgement of my heart is tide?
Why fhould my heart thinke that a feuerall plot,
Which my heart knowes the wide worlds common place?
Or mine eyes feeing this,fay this is not
To put faire truth vpon fo foule a face,
   In things right true my heart:and eyes haue erred,
   And to this falfe plague are they now transferred.

138

WHen my loue fweares that fhe is made of truth,
   I do beleeue her though I know fhe lyes,
That fhe might thinke me fome vntuterd youth,
Vnlearned in the worlds falfe fubtilties.
Thus vainely thinking that fhe thinkes me young,
Although fhe knowes my dayes are paft the beft,
Simply I credit her falfe fpeaking tongue,
On both fides thus is fimple truth fuppreft:
But wherefore fayes fhe not fhe is vniuft?
And wherefore fay not I that I am old?
O loues beft habit is in feeming truft,
And age in loue,loues not t'haue yeares told.
   Therefore I lye with her,and fhe with me,
   And in our faults by lyes we flattered be.

139

OCall not me to iuftifie the wrong,
   That thy vnkindneffe layes vpon my heart,
Wound me not with thine eye but with thy toung,
Vfe power with power,and flay me not by Art,
Tell me thou lou'ft elfe-where;but in my fight,
Deare heart forbeare to glance thine eye afide,
What needft thou wound with cunning when thy might

Is

Is more then my ore-prest defence can bide?
Let me excuse thee,ah my loue well knowes,
Her prettie lookes haue beene mine enemies,
And therefore from my face she turnes my foes,
That they else-where might dart their iniuries:
  Yet do not so,but since I am neere slaine,
  Kill me out-right with lookes,and rid my paine.

140

BE wise as thou art cruell,do not presse
  My toung-tide patience with too much disdaine:
Least sorrow lend me words and words expresse,
The manner of my pittie wanting paine.
If I might teach thee witte better it weare,
Though not to loue,yet loue to tell me so,
As testie sick-men when their deaths be neere,
No newes but health from their Phisitions know.
For if I should dispaire I should grow madde,
And in my madnesse might speake ill of thee,
Now this ill wresting world is growne so bad,
Madde slanderers by madde eares beleeued:be.
  That I may not be so, nor thou be lyde,   (wide.
  Beare thine eyes straight, though thy proud heart goe

141

IN faith I doe not loue thee with mine eyes,
  For they in thee a thousand errors note,
But 'tis my heart that loues what they dispise,
Who in dispight of view is pleasd to dote.
Nor are mine eares with thy toungs tune delighted,
Nor tender feeling to base touches prone,
Nor taste, nor smell, desire to be inuited
To any sensuall feast with thee alone:
But my fiue wits,nor my fiue sences can
Diswade one foolish heart from seruing thee,
Who leaues vnswai'd the likenesse of a man,
Thy proud hearts slaue and vassall wretch to be:
  Onely my plague thus farre I count my gaine,
  That she that makes me sinne,awards me paine.

I 2   Loue

142

LOue is my sinne, and thy deare vertue hate,
Hate of my sinne, grounded on sinfull louing,
O but with mine, compare thou thine owne state,
And thou shalt finde it merrits not reproouing,
Or if it do, not from those lips of thine,
That haue prophan'd their scarlet ornaments,
And seald false bonds of loue as oft as mine,
Robd others beds reuenues of their rents.
Be it lawfull I loue thee as thou lou'st those,
Whome thine eyes wooe as mine importune thee,
Roote pittie in thy heart that when it growes,
Thy pitty may deserue to pittied bee.
   If thou doost seeke to haue what thou doost hide,
   By selfe example mai'st thou be denide.

143

LOe as a carefull huswife runnes to catch,
One of her fethered creatures broake away,
Sets downe her babe and makes all swift dispatch
In pursuit of the thing she would haue stay:
Whilst her neglected child holds her in chace,
Cries to catch her whose busie care is bent,
To follow that which flies before her face:
Not prizing her poore infants discontent;
So runst thou after that which flies from thee,
Whilst I thy babe chace thee a farre behind,
But if thou catch thy hope turne back to me:
And play the mothers part kisse me, be kind.
   So will I pray that thou maist haue thy *Will*,
   If thou turne back and my loude crying still.

144

TWo loues I haue of comfort and dispaire,
Which like two spirits do sugiest me still,
The better angell is a man right faire:
The worser spirit a woman collour'd il.
To win me soone to hell my femall euill,

Tempteth

Tempteth my better angel from my sight,
And would corrupt my saint to be a diuel:
Wooing his purity with her fowle pride.
And whether that my angel be turn'd finde,
Suspect I may, yet not directly tell,
But being both from me both to each friend,
I geſſe one angel in an others hel.

   Yet this ſhal I nere know but liue in doubt,
    Till my bad angel fire my good one out.

145

THoſe lips that Loues owne hand did make,
  Breath'd forth the ſound that ſaid I hate,
To me that languiſht for her ſake:
But when ſhe ſaw my wofull ſtate,
Straight in her heart did mercie come,
Chiding that tongue that euer ſweet,
Was vſde in giuing gentle dome:
And tought it thus a new to greete:
I hate ſhe alterd with an end,
That follow'd it as gentle day,
Doth follow night who like a fiend
From heauen to hell is flowne away.

   I hate, from hate away ſhe threw,
    And ſau'd my life ſaying not you.

146

POore ſoule the center of my ſinfull earth,
  My ſinfull earth theſe rebbell powres that thee array,
Why doſt thou pine within and ſuffer dearth,
Painting thy outward walls ſo coſtlie gay?
Why ſo large coſt hauing ſo ſhort a leaſe,
Doſt thou vpon thy fading manſion ſpend?
Shall wormes inheritors of this exceſſe,
Eate vp thy charge? is this thy bodies end?
Then ſoule liue thou vpon thy ſeruants loſſe,
And let that pine to aggrauat thy ſtore;
Buy tearmes diuine in ſelling houres of droſſe:

                       Within

Within be fed, without be rich no more,
So shalt thou feed on death, that feeds on men,
And death once dead, ther's no more dying then.

147

MY loue is as a feauer longing still,
For that which longer nurseth the disease,
Feeding on that which doth preserue the ill,
Th'vncertaine sicklie appetite to please:
My reason the Phisition to my loue,
Angry that his prescriptions are not kept
Hath left me, and I desperate now approoue,
Desire is death, which Phisick did except.
Past cure I am, now Reason is past care,
And frantick madde with euer-more vnrest,
My thoughts and my discourse as mad mens are,
At randon from the truth vainely exprest.
    For I haue sworne thee faire, and thought thee bright,
    Who art as black as hell, as darke as night.

148

O Me! what eyes hath loue put in my head,
Which haue no correspondence with true sight,
Or if they haue, where is my iudgment fled,
That censures falsely what they see aright?
If that be faire whereon my false eyes dote,
What meanes the world to say it is not so?
If it be not, then loue doth well denote,
Loues eye is not so true as all mens:no,
How can it? O how can loues eye be true,
That is so vext with watching and with teares?
No maruaile then though I mistake my view,
The sunne it selfe sees not, till heauen cleeres.
    O cunning loue, with teares thou keepst me blinde,
    Least eyes well seeing thy foule faults should finde.

149

CAnst thou O cruell, say I loue thee not,
When I against my selfe with thee pertake:

Doe

Doe I not thinke on thee when I forgot
Am of my selfe, all tirant for thy sake?
Who hateth thee that I doe call my friend,
On whom froun'st thou that I doe faune vpon,
Nay if thou lowrst on me doe I not spend
Reuenge vpon my selfe with present mone?
What merrit do I in my selfe respect,
That is so proude thy seruice to dispise,
When all my best doth worship thy defect,
Commanded by the motion of thine eyes.
   But loue hate on for now I know thy minde,
   Those that can see thou lou'st, and I am blind.

150

OH from what powre hast thou this powrefull might,
  With insufficiency my heart to sway,
To make me giue the lie to my true sight,
And swere that brightnesse doth not grace the day?
Whence hast thou this becomming of things il,
That in the very refuse of thy deeds,
There is such strength and warranti e of skill,
That in my minde thy worst all best exceeds?
Who taught thee how to make me loue thee more,
The more I heare and see iust cause of hate,
Oh though I loue what others doe abhor,
VVith others thou shouldst not abhor my state.
   If thy vnworthinesse raisd loue in me,
   More worthy I to be belou'd of thee.

151

LOue is too young to know what conscience is,
  Yet who knowes not conscience is borne of loue,
Then gentle cheater vrge not my amisse,
Leaft guilty of my faults thy sweet selfe proue.
For thou betraying me, I doe betray
My nobler part to my grose bodies treason,
My soule doth tell my body that he may,
Triumph in loue, flesh staies no farther reason,
                     But

But ryfing at thy name doth point out thee,
As his triumphant prize,proud of this pride,
He is contented thy poore drudge to be
To ftand in thy affaires,fall by thy fide.
   No want of confcience hold it that I call,
   Her loue,for whofe deare loue I rife and fall.

152

IN louing thee thou know'ft I am forfworne,
But thou art twice forfworne to me loue fwearing,
In act thy bed-vow broake and new faith torne,
In vowing new hate after new loue bearing:
But why of two othes breach doe I accufe thee,
When I breake twenty:I am periur'd moft,
For all my vowes are othes but to mifufe thee:
And all my honeft faith in thee is loft.
For I haue fworne deepe othes of thy deepe kindneffe:
Othes of thy loue,thy truth,thy conftancie,
And to inlighten thee gaue eyes to blindneffe,
Or made them fwere againft the thing they fee.
   For I haue fworne thee faire:more periurde eye,
   To fwere againft the truth fo foule a lie.

153

CVpid laid by his brand and fell a fleepe,
A maide of Dyans this aduantage found,
And his loue-kindling fire did quickly fteepe
In a could vallie-fountaine of that ground:
Which borrowd from this holie fire of loue,
A dateleffe liuely heat ftill to indure,
And grew a feething bath which yet men proue,
Againft ftrang malladies a foueraigne cure:
But at my miftres eie loues brand new fired,
The boy for triall needes would touch my breft,
I fick withall the helpe of bath defired,
And thether hied a fad diftemperd gueft.
   But found no cure,the bath for my helpe lies,
   Where Cupid got new fire;my miftres eye.

154

THe little Loue-God lying once a ſleepe,
Laid by his ſide his heart inflaming brand,
Whilſt many Nymphes that vou'd chaſt life to keep,
Came tripping by, but in her maiden hand,
The fayreſt votary tooke vp that fire,
Which many Legions of true hearts had warm'd,
And ſo the Generall of hot deſire,
Was ſleeping by a Virgin hand diſarm'd.
This brand ſhe quenched in a coole Well by,
Which from loues fire tooke heat perpetuall,
Growing a bath and healthfull remedy,
For men diſeaſd, but I my Miſtriſſe thrall,
 Came there for cure and this by that I proue,
 Loues fire heates water, water cooles not loue.

FINIS.

A Louers complaint.

BY

WILLIAM SHAKE-SPEARE.

FRom off a hill whose concaue wombe reworded,
A plaintfull story from a sistring vale
My spirrits t'attend this doble voyce accorded,
And downe I laid to list the sad tun'd tale,
Ere long espied a sickle maid full pale
Tearing of papers breaking rings a twaine,
Storming her world with sorrowes, wind and raine.

Vpon her head a plattid hiue of straw,
Which fortified her visage from the Sunne,
Whereon the thought might thinke sometime it saw
The carkas of a beauty spent and donne,
Time had not sithed all that youth begun,
Nor youth all quit, but spight of heauens fell rage,
Some beauty peept, through lettice of sear'd age.

Oft did she heaue her Napkin to her eyne,
Which on it had conceited charecters:
Laundring the silken figures in the brine,
That seasoned woe had pelleted in teares,
And often reading what contents it beares:
As often shriking vndistinguisht wo,
In clamours of all size both high and low,

Some-times her leueld eyes their carriage ride,
As they did battry to the spheres intend:
Sometime diuerted their poore balls are tide,
To th'orbed earth; sometimes they do extend,
Their view right on, anon their gases lend,

To.

To euery place at once and no where fixt,
The mind and fight diftractedly commxit.

Her haire nor loofe nor ti'd in formall plat,
Proclaimd in her a carelefle hand of pride;
For fome vntuck'd defcended her fheu'd hat,
Hanging her pale and pined cheeke befide,
Some in her threeden fillet ftill did bide,
And trew to bondage would not breake from thence,
Though flackly braided in loofe negligence.

A thoufand fauours from a maund fhe drew,
Of amber chriftall and of bedded Iet,
Which one by one fhe in a riuer threw,
Vpon whofe weeping margent fhe was fet,
Like vfery applying wet to wet,
Or Monarches hands that lets not bounty fall,
Where want cries fome; but where exceffe begs all.

Of folded fchedulls had fhe many a one,
Which fhe peruf d, fighd, tore and gaue the flud,
Crackt many a ring of Pofied gold and bone,
Bidding them find their Sepulchers in mud,
Found yet mo letters fadly pend in blood,
With fleided filke, feate and affectedly
Enfwath'd and feald to curious fecrecy.

Thefe often bath'd fhe in her fluxiue eies,
And often kift, and often gaue to teare,
Cried O falfe blood thou regifter of lies,
What vnapproued witnes dooft thou beare!
Inke would haue feem'd more blacke and damned heare!
This faid in top of rage the lines fhe rents,
Big difcontent, fo breaking their contents.

A reuerend man that graz'd his cattell ny,

K 2   Some

Sometime a blusterer that the ruffle knew
Of Court of Cittie, and had let go by
The swiftest houres obserued as they flew,
Towards this afflicted fancy fastly drew:
And priuiledg'd by age desires to know
In breefe the grounds and motiues of her wo.

So slides he downe vppon his greyned bat;
And comely distant sits he by her side,
When hee againe desires her, being satte,
Her greeuance with his hearing to deuide:
If that from him there may be ought applied
Which may her suffering extasie asswage
Tis promist in the charitie of age.

Father she saies, though in mee you behold
The iniury of many a blasting houre;
Let it not tell your Iudgement I am old,
Not age, but sorrow, ouer me hath power;
I might as yet haue bene a spreading flower
Fresh to my selfe, if I had selfe applyed
Loue to my selfe, and to no Loue beside.

But wo is mee, too early I atttended
A youthfull suit it was to gaine my grace;
O one by natures outwards so commended,
That maidens eyes stucke ouer all his face,
Loue lackt a dwelling and made him her place.
And when in his faire parts shee didde abide,
Shee was new lodg'd and newly Deified.

His browny locks did hang in crooked curles,
And euery light occasion of the wind
Vpon his lippes their silken parcels hurles,
Whats sweet to do, to do wil aptly find,
Each eye that saw him did inchaunt the minde:

For

For on his vifage was in little drawne,
What largeneffe thinkes in parradife was fawne.

Smal fhew of man was yet vpon his chinne,
His phenix downe began but to appeare
Like vnfhorne veluet, on that termleffe skin
Whofe bare out-brag'd the web it feem'd to were,
Yet fhewed his vifage by that coft more deare,
And nice affections wauering ftood in doubt
If beft were as it was, or beft without.

His qualities were beautious as his forme,
For maiden tongu'd he was and thereof free;
Yet if men mou'd him, was he fuch a ftorme
As oft twixt May and Aprill is to fee,
When windes breath fweet, vnruly though they bee.
His rudeneffe fo with his authoriz'd youth,
Did liuery falfeneffe in a pride of truth.

Wel could hee ride, and often men would fay
That horfe his mettell from his rider takes
Proud of fubiection, noble by the fwaie,   (makes
What rounds, what bounds, what courfe what ftop he
And controuerfie hence a queftion takes,
Whether the horfe by him became his deed,
Or he his mannad'g, by'th wel doing Steed.

But quickly on this fide the verdict went,
His reall habitude gaue life and grace
To appertainings and to ornament,
Accomplifht in him-felfe not in his cafe:
All ayds them-felues made fairer by their place,
Can for addicions, yet their purpof'd trimme
Peec'd not his grace but were al grac'd by him.

So on the tip of his fubduing tongue

K 3   All

All kinde of arguments and question deepe,
Al replication prompt, and reason strong
For his aduantage still did wake and sleep,
To make the weeper laugh, the laugher weepe:
He had the dialect and different skil,
Catching al passions in his craft of will.

That hee didde in the general bosome raigne
Of young, of old, and sexes both inchanted,
To dwel with him in thoughts, or to remaine
In personal duty, following where he haunted,
Consent's bewitcht, ere he desire haue granted,
And dialogu'd for him what he would say,
Askt their own wils and made their wils obey.

Many there were that did his picture gette
To serue their eies, and in it put their mind,
Like fooles that in th' imagination set
The goodly obiects which abroad they find
Of lands and mansions, theirs in thought assign'd,
And labouring in moe pleasures to bestow them,
Then the true gouty Land-lord which doth owe them.

So many haue that neuer toucht his hand
Sweetly suppos'd them mistresse of his hearte:
My wofull selfe that did in freedome stand,
And was my owne fee simple (not in part)
What with his art in youth and youth in art
Threw my affections in his charmed power,
Reseru'd the stalke and gaue him al my flower.

Yet did I not as some my equals did
Demaund of him, nor being desired yeelded,
Finding my selfe in honour so forbidde,
With safest distance I mine honour sheelded,
Experience for me many bulwarkes builded

of

Of proofs new bleeding which remaind the foile
Of this false Iewell, and his amorous spoile.

But ah who euer shun'd by precedent,
The destin'd ill she must her selfe assay,
Or forc'd examples gainst her owne content
To put the by-past perrils in her way?
Counsaile may stop a while what will not stay:
For when we rage, aduise is often seene
By blunting vs to make our wits more keene.

Nor giues it satisfaction to our blood,
That wee must curbe it vppon others proofe,
To be forbod the sweets that seemes so good,
For feare of harmes that preach in our behoofe;
O appetite from iudgement stand aloofe!
The one a pallate hath that needs will taste,
Though reason weepe and cry it is thy last.

For further I could say this mans vntrue,
And knew the patternes of his foule beguiling,
Heard where his plants in others Orchards grew,
Saw how deceits were guilded in his smiling,
Knew vowes, were euer brokers to defiling,
Thought Characters and words meerly but art,
And bastards of his foule adulterat heart.

And long vpon these termes I held my Citty,
Till thus hee gan besiege me : Gentle maid
Haue of my suffering youth some feeling pitty,
And be not of my holy vowes affraid,
Thats to ye sworne to none was euer said,
For feasts of loue I haue bene call'd vnto
Till now did nere inuite nor neuer vovv.

All my offences that abroad you see

Are

Are errors of the blood none of the mind:
Loue made them not, with acture they may be,
Where neither Party is nor trew nor kind,
They sought their shame that so their shame did find,
And so much lesse of shame in me remaines,
By how much of me their reproch containes,

Among the many that mine eyes haue seene,
Not one whose flame my hart so much as warmed,
Or my affection put to th, smallest teene,
Or any of my leisures euer Charmed,
Harme haue I done to them but nere was harmed,
Kept hearts in liueries, but mine owne was free,
And raignd commaunding in his monarchy.

Looke heare what tributes wounded fancies sent me,
Of palyd pearles and rubies red as blood:
Figuring that they their passions likewise lent me
Of greefe and blushes, aptly vnderstood
In bloodlesse white, and the encrimson'd mood,
Effects of terror and deare modesty,
Encampt in hearts but fighting outwardly.

And Lo behold these tallents of their heir,
With twisted mettle amoroufly empleacht
I haue receau'd from many a seueral faire,
Their kind acceptance, wepingly befeecht,
With th'annexions of faire gems inricht,
And deepe brain'd sonnets that did amplifie
Each stones deare Nature, worth and quallity.

The Diamond? why twas beautifull and hard,
Whereto his inuis'd properties did tend,
The deepe greene Emrald in whose fresh regard,
Weake sights their sickly radience do amend,
The heauen hewd Saphir and the Opall blend

With

With obiects manyfold ; each seuerall stone,
With wit well blazond smil'd or made some mone.

Lo all these trophies of affections hot,
Of pensiu'd and subdew'd desires the tender,
Nature hath chargd me that I hoord them not,
But yeeld them vp where I my selfe must render:
That is to you my origin and ender :
For these of force must your oblations be,
Since I their Aulter, you enpatrone me.

Oh then aduance(of yours)that phraseles hand,
Whose white weighes downe the airy scale of praise,
Take all these similies to your owne command,
Hollowed with sighes that burning lunges did raise:
What me your minister for you obaies
Workes vnder you,and to your audit comes
Their distract parcells,in combined summes.

Lo this deuice was sent me from a Nun,
Or Sister sanctified of holiest note,
Which late her noble suit in court did shun,
Whose rarest hauings made the blossoms dote,
For she was sought by spirits of ritchest cote,
But kept cold distance,and did thence remoue,
To spend her liuing in eternall loue.

But oh my sweet what labour ist to leaue,
The thing we haue not,mastring what not striues,
Playing the Place which did no forme receiue,
Playing patient sports in vnconstraind giues,
She that her fame so to her selfe contriues,
The scarres of bartaile scapeth by the flight,
And makes her absence valiant,not her might.

Oh pardon me in that my boast is true,

L   The

The accident which brought me to her eie,
Vpon the moment did her force subdewe,
And now she would the caged cloister flie:
Religious loue put out religions eye:
Not to be tempted would she be enur'd,
And now to tempt all liberty procure.

How mightie then you are, Oh heare me tell,
The broken bosoms that to me belong,
Haue emptied all their fountaines in my wells:
And mine I powre your Ocean all amonge:
I strong ore them and you ore me being strong,
Must for your victorie vs all congest,
As compound loue to phisick your cold brest.

My parts had powre to charme a sacred Sunne,
Who disciplin'd I dieted in grace,
Beleeu'd her eies, when they t' assaile begun,
All vowes and consecrations giuing place:
O most potentiall loue, vowe, bond, nor space
In thee hath neither sting, knot, nor confine
For thou art all and all things els are thine.

When thou impressest what are precepts worth
Of stale example? when thou wilt inflame,
How coldly those impediments stand forth
Of wealth of filliall feare, lawe, kindred fame,   (shame
Loues armes are peace, gainst rule, gainst sence, gainst
And sweetens in the suffring pangues it beares,
The *Alloes* of all forces, shockes and feares.

Now all these hearts that doe on mine depend,
Feeling it breake, with bleeding groanes they pine,
And supplicant their sighes to you extend
To leaue the battrie that you make gainst mine,
Lending soft audience, to my sweet designe,

And

And credent foule, to that strong bonded oth,
That shall preferre and vndertake my troth.

This said, his watrie eies he did difmount,
Whofe fightes till then were leaueld on my face,
Each cheeke a riuer running from a fount,
With brynifh currant downe-ward flowed a pace:
Oh how the channell to the ftreame gaue grace!
Who glaz'd with Chriftail gate the glowing Rofes,
That flame through water which their hew incloſes,

Oh father, what a heil of witch-craft lies,
In the fmall orb of one perticular teare?
But with the invndation of the eies:
What rocky heart to water will not weare?
What breft fo cold that is not warmed heare,
Or cleft effect, cold modefly hot wrath:
Both fire from hence, and chill extincture hath.

For loe his paffion but an art of craft,
Euen there refolu'd my reafon into teares,
There my white ftole of chaftity I daft,
Shooke off my fober gardes, and ciuill feares,
Appeare to him as he to me appeares:
All melting, though our drops this diffrence bore,
His poifon'd me, and mine did him reftore.

In him a plenitude of fubtle matter,
Applied to Cautills, all ftraing formes receiues,
Of burning blufhes, or of weeping water,
Or founding paleneffe: and he takes and leaues,
In eithers aptneffe as it beft deceiues:
To blufh at fpeeches ranck, to weepe at woes
Or to turne white and found at tragick fhowes.

That not a heart which in his leuell came,
L 3 Could

Could scape the haile of his all hurting ayme,
Shewing faire Nature is both kinde and tame:
And vaild in them did winne whom he would maime,
Against the thing he sought,he would exclaime,
When he most burnt in hart-wisht luxurie,
He preacht pure maide,and praisd cold chastitie.

Thus meerely with the garment of a grace,
The naked and concealed feind he couerd,
That th'vnexperient gaue the tempter place,
Which like a Cherubin aboue them houerd,
Who young and simple would not be so louerd.
Aye me I fell,and yet do question make,
What I should doe againe for such a sake.

O that infected moysture of his eye,
O that false fire which in his cheeke so glowd:
O that forc'd thunder from his heart did flye,
O that sad breath his spungie lungs bestowed,
O all that borrowed motion seeming owed,
Would yet againe betray the fore-betrayed,
And new peruert a reconciled Maide.

FINIS.